Gintare Sutkauskaite

Improvement of social media communication for fashion brand

GW00457601

Gintare Sutkauskaite

Improvement of social media communication for fashion brand

Aiming to increase brand awareness and involvement

Scholar's Press

Impressum / Imprint
Bibliografische Information der Deutschen Nationalbibliothek: Die Deutsche Nationalbibliothek verzeichnet diese Publikation in der Deutschen Nationalbibliografie; detaillierte bibliografische Daten sind im Internet über http://dnb.d-nb.de abrufbar.
Alle in diesem Buch genannten Marken und Produktnamen unterliegen warenzeichen-, marken- oder patentrechtlichem Schutz bzw. sind Warenzeichen oder eingetragene Warenzeichen der jeweiligen Inhaber. Die Wiedergabe von Marken, Produktnamen, Gebrauchsnamen, Handelsnamen, Warenbezeichnungen u.s.w. in diesem Werk berechtigt auch ohne besondere Kennzeichnung nicht zu der Annahme, dass solche Namen im Sinne der Warenzeichen- und Markenschutzgesetzgebung als frei zu betrachten wären und daher von jedermann benutzt werden dürften.

Bibliographic information published by the Deutsche Nationalbibliothek: The Deutsche Nationalbibliothek lists this publication in the Deutsche Nationalbibliografie; detailed bibliographic data are available in the Internet at http://dnb.d-nb.de.
Any brand names and product names mentioned in this book are subject to trademark, brand or patent protection and are trademarks or registered trademarks of their respective holders. The use of brand names, product names, common names, trade names, product descriptions etc. even without a particular marking in this work is in no way to be construed to mean that such names may be regarded as unrestricted in respect of trademark and brand protection legislation and could thus be used by anyone.

Coverbild / Cover image: www.ingimage.com

Verlag / Publisher:
Scholar's Press
ist ein Imprint der / is a trademark of
OmniScriptum GmbH & Co. KG
Heinrich-Böcking-Str. 6-8, 66121 Saarbrücken, Deutschland / Germany
Email: info@scholars-press.com

Herstellung: siehe letzte Seite /
Printed at: see last page
ISBN: 978-3-639-76422-2

Abstract

Sutkauskaite G., Improvement of social media communication for fashion brand in Latvian market.

The importance of social media not only for individuals but for businesses as well, keeps increasing constantly. It prompts that companies have to revise their communication strategies and consider the dominance of social media platforms in order to increase brand awareness and involvement. Therefore, work is based on Lithuanian retail giant company's brand that was launched particularly for Latvian market. The aim is to develop communication plan through social media and identify steps that would result in improvement of interaction with current and potential customers. Quantitative empirical research was employed in order to reveal factors that would affect target customer's involvement with a brand on social media spaces. Survey was provided in online questionnaire form, distributing it for Riga's and it's region residents that fits in age range of 25-34. Based on overview of academical literature and results of conducted quantitaive reasearch, managerial solutions for social media communication plan improvement will be delivered. The most important findings suggest that brand Z has to engage more with local Latvian social networking platforms and comunication has to be orientated more towards educational and entertaining activities. Moreover as vast majority of respondents falls into critics and joiners/spectators behavioral types, content has to provide opportunity to share reviews and encourage discussions.

Keywords: social media plan, communication improvement, clothing retail business, retail in Baltic States region, brand awareness and involvement.

Table of Contents

List of Tables

List of Figures

IMPROVEMENT OF SOCIAL MEDIA COMMUNICATION

5

IMPROVEMENT OF SOCIAL MEDIA COMMUNICATION

Introduction

Relevance of the topic. Companies of all kinds, starting from consumer product manufacturers to banks and non-profit organizations – all have to use marketing and communication strategies in order to understand their customer and grow their business. Even the giant companies like ZARA or BMW can not afford to relax their marketing effort if they want to defend their leading positions within a market. (Kotler, 2009, p. 4)

In this fast pace environment old marketing methods, like interruption marketing is in permanent decline, while new waves of communication techniques are booming. Social media grow across different environments resulting fundamental changes in society, technology and business practices. Social spaces provide opportunity for business not only to spread their message, but to get a feedback on it while communicating their brand directly and personally.

Lithuanian based joint-stock company X is a distinct leader of clothing industry in Baltic States. Currently, company is holding approximately 35% of total market share within local - Lithuanian market and about 20% in Latvia. As company is mostly operating through franchising system, marketing decisions are not made fully by the company X itself for brands that are held under franchising agreements.

However, company X continuously invests money and resources in order to improve customer's involvement with their own trademarks. They apply many traditional marketing strategies, while digital platforms are not company's forte so far. Even though both company's X brands that are orientated towards youth segment – brand Y in Lithuania and brand Z in Latvia are already using social media platforms, it is still hard to assess positive impact on overall company's performance. Noticeable difference between these two is that brand Y today has approximately 34.500 followers on their Facebook page, while alternative brand for youth segment in Latvia –brand Z has only 1202 followers. Therefore, this work will be based on

6

improvement of communication through social media for youth brand Z, which would help to strengthen customer relationships and increase brand awareness as well.

Consequently, the **research problem** is the following: What actions should be taken to improve communication through social media for brand Z in order to increase brand awareness and involvement?

The **aim** is to develop communication plan through social media and identify actions that would result in improvement of communication with current and potential customers.

In order to reach the aim, following **objectives** have been raised:

Make internal and external analysis of the company and particularly their brand Z in Latvian market;

To accomplish quantitative empirical research in order to identify what would encourage engagement with brand Z among age group of 25-34 in social media;

To provide managerial solutions for improvement of communication plan through social media of brand Z for 2015.

Research methods. Analysis and interpretation of academic literature, quantitative empirical research collected in questionnaires form, interpretation of secondary data.

Practical value of the thesis. Results of empirical research showed what activities are the most attractive and relevant for brand's target market within social media platform. Managerial solutions suggests how to attract more target market to brand's social media channels and make communication more interactive at the same time increasing brand awareness.

Logical sequence. Work is structured in the following way:

- *Introduction* which provides formulated problem and the overall objectives;

7

- *Situational analysis.* General information of the company is provided together with internal and external environmental analysis;

- *Empirical research.* In this part research method is selected and process of research is described in detail. Later on, results are systemized and conclusions are made;

- *Managerial solutions.* The solutions of the raised problem are provided, suggesting what steps should be made in order to improve overall performance of brand's communication through social media;

- *Conclusions* of the thesis.

Current Situation Analysis

This part is aimed at presenting current situation of company X and particularly their brand Z which is representing youth segment in Latvian market. Internal analysis is made using marketing communications mix tool and having deeper look into marketing strategies of brand Z within Latvian market. While external company's analysis is explained through PESTEL model and by analyzing current industry situation in Latvia. Situation analysis is conducted in order to identify problem and prove its importance for the company.

Internal Analysis

Today company X is leading clothing retailer in Baltic States. Nevertheless it took 69 years to build an empire that today holds 158 stores in 3 countries, works with 33 well known brands and serves 5 totally different market segments. Company mainly operates under franchising agreements and is a representative in Baltic States of globally known brands such as Zara, Massimo Dutti, Bershka, Emporio Armani, Hugo Boss to mention just a few. Moreover, company X steers 5 trademarks established on their own. Production sold in stores that company X owns today is manufactured in Lithuania, Poland, the Far East and Italy.

Company is segmenting their market to 5 very different segments - economic segment (targeting families), youth segment, business segment, luxury segment, ZARA shops and outlet stores.

Now there are 96 stores in Lithuania, 44 – in Latvia and 18 – in Estonia. One of the core missions within a company is to not accept compromises while selecting best locations for store operations. So all the stores are located in the best places, assuring that the highest European standards and technologies are applied.

This work will be concentrated on particular brand Z that is private trademark of company X. As these stores are orientated towards youth segment, it is important

9

to mention that so far it is the most profitable segment for the company, which brings approximately 33.7% of overall profits. (See Appendix No 1.) Brand Z stores offers clothes and accessories for man and women of famous brands like Diesel, Miss Sixty, Energy, Broadway, Morgan or Jack&Jones. First store was opened in Riga on 2005 and today there are already 2 stores opened.

Originally brand Z stores were created in Latvian market as substitute for brand Y in Lithuania and it was expected to replicate last-mentioned success. Unfortunately, process of entering market was not as successful as expected therefore it took 9 years to open doors of second brand Z store in Riga. Today both stores are located in one of the biggest shopping centers of Riga: Riga Plaza and Galleria Riga.

There were several reasons explaining why the same concept did not work in neighbour countries. First of all, as brand Y contained the name of the company itself, which was well known within Lithuanian market for 69 years and through the whole years of experience had earn trust and appreciation, it was a lot easier to build strong brand for youth segment afterwards. While brand Z name did not had any previous associations within Latvian market, so back then, on 2005 it was totally new brand, which needed lots of investments in marketing and communications in order to build trust and status. Moreover when brand Z was established, company was focused on gaining and strengthening market position in Lithuania, while business in other Baltic States were on secondary focus. Especially when on 2007 sales stopped increasing in Latvian market and it was hard to forecast future situation, company was not adapting any aggressive expansion strategies within this market. Therefore, brand Z did not expand till 1st quarter of 2014.

Marketing communications mix of brand Z. Marketing communications mix is a tool providing menu of communication methods that are most ideally used blended. Marketing communications mix usually comprises advertising, public relations, direct marketing, sales and promotional activities.

(Dahlen, Lange and Smith, 2010, p. 277). Today one more very important distinct area is added to marketing communication mix – digital marketing and e-commerce.

Advertising. One of the major missions of company X is to be first in the market. Consequently company adapts its advertising campaigns in the way to be positioned on customer's mind as "first". Significant amount of whole marketing budget falls into advertising function. Whole marketing budget for the company X, according to consolidated annual report (2013, p. 24) last year was equal to 1 642 898 EUR, what is approximately 136 908 EUR/month. Budget is divided between advertising methods by professional agencies in order to achieve the very best outcome.

Overall print media consumption today in Latvia is at a very high level. Advertisements of brand Z are continuously placed within most popular magazines like „Cosmopolitan", "Privata Dzive", "Klubs" and "Ieva", as well as in specialized shopping centers magazines. TV advertising was not used so far for this particular brand, as it is not the best tool to reach youth audience today. Moreover as there are only 2 stores opened, not a big portion of overall company's resources is invested in the promotion of this particular brand.

Direct marketing. As one of the biggest advantages of this method, Bhattacharya, C. (2006, p.310) highlighted customer's loyalty building being more effective through the initiation of a dialogue rather than reaching customers by mass media monologues. Brand Z applies this method by collecting post-purchase surveys containing customer's name, surname, phone number and email. In this case, sales person within a store works as intermediary assuring if the customer is willing to get more information on sales straight to their emails. This is how permission marketing technique is applied by brand Z and many other brands that belongs to this company. Eventually, all filled in forms with target audience's personal data are archived and

11

later used for more individualized communication in this way building stronger ties with loyal customers.

Public relations. Even though, according to Moss, Warnaby and Thame (1996, p. 73) it is strongly suggested to separate public relations function from marketing within a company – company X practices public relations within the same marketing department. In order to strengthen public relations, company is organizing events to create strong fashion community and at the same time to communicate their brand message. On April 21 of 2014, company organized public relations event dedicated for brand Z in one of the busiest night clubs in Riga city – „Mai Tai". The party idea was to bring all fashion youth and in this way increase brand awareness. Event was successful as it gathered a lot of fashion involved Latvian youth. Club was decorated with brand logos and with the help of promotional crew brand's persona was embodied.

Sales promotions. Discounts and promotions are essential part of clothing industry. All big sales are usually promoted through paid communication and by changing displays of the stores to call customer's attention towards discounts. During the last months of the season, brand Z stores are calling customers to check discounts within store, while placing huge displays with discounts that sometimes counts up to 70%. This form of communication is aimed to increase revenues, at the same time attracting new customers and clearing out inventory.

Digital marketing and e-commerce. Brand Z do not practice selling their goods via digital channels so far, however company is already trying to communicate with target audience employing social media spaces. It is inevitable as today's youth simply grew up with social media and feel with it as comfortable as older generation with traditional marketing forms such as television. (Sweeney, Craig, 2011, p.13) Although brand's Z social media communication is so far at its early phase. As Facebook page of this brand was created on 2011 and today has only 1120 followers.

Moreover brand has its fan page on local – draugiem.lv social network, although they did not start any activities in there yet.

Major brand Z activities on social media spaces are posts picturing clothes from new collections. Even though this is very common content to see on any social media page of fashion brand, brand Z differentiates presenting clothes worn by casual person in store rather than catwalk model on eye catching advertisement. Moreover, fan page accommodates some promotional videos and motivational quotes. Unfortunatelly, so far page is not very hectic, as interest to all page's activities is relatively low and followers are not engaged with any discussions or sharing.

Moreover, on the digital area company X placed their official website, which is available in 3 languages and contains information forwarded to customers, investors and press. The site was newly restored in 2014 and now is providing more options than before.

One of the major goals for offline business when it comes to advertising is to entice the customer to visit the store. (Augostino, 2007, p.10) Social media can be used as a free tool to reach your target customers and send them a message that would encourage get off the computer and go straight into the store.

External Analysis

External analysis is aimed to ascertain portrait of target customers, evaluate competitive landscape and identify certain trends that impact business activities.

Market Segmentation. According to Gunter and Furnham (1992) one of key elements in modern marketing is market division, based on demographical, geographical, psychological and behavioral factors. When we are talking about clothing industry, markets are usually segmented according to demographical factors, such as gender, age and most importantly income. Alike it is important to consider behavioral factors that usually play very important role in clothing industry, as in most cases people tend to make purchasing decisions impulsively rather than rationally.

Brand Z particularly is orientated towards youth segment and their slogan states „Brand Z - for youth who has their own lifestyle". This particular market segment is referred to a "fashionable youth" and more precisely for the ones who get higher than average income. As according to Household budget survey compiled by Central Statistical Bureau of Latvia (2014), despite the fact that household consumption expenditure has grown by 6.7% last year, Latvians on average spend 17.41EUR/month on clothing and footwear. Therefore stores are orientated towards customers getting average (815Eur in Riga) or higher income. (Latvijas Statistika, 2014)

Brand Z market segment characteristics:

- Age range 24- 35 years, as other company's segments are orientated towards audience of 18-25 years old;

- Riga and its region citizens;

- Having average and higher income, as price range fluctuates from 40 – 140Eur for a dress;

- Value more brand name than functionality of clothes itself;

- Express their personality through clothing style;

- Fashion involved, sensible for trends.

Brand Z stores are not focusing on women's apparel only, as part of the store is dedicated for masculine collections. Specific thing about youth segment - is a generation, that could be easily affected by social media or saying in other words – by instinct "to follow the mass". Consequently their decision making can be influenced by highlighting huge sales in stores or spreading out the marketing message through social media platforms.

To sum everything up, one of the most important questions for every company remains how to reach their audience and translate their message most effectively.

14

While young people today are victims of digital generation, they are exploring the world without leaving home. According to Eurostat (2009 p. 138-160) 61% of Latvian residents aged 25-34, what is brand Z target audience, use internet every day. Moreover, biggest percentage – 86% of this age group are using internet access for finding information about goods and services. (See Appendix No 2 for internet activites by age group) Therefore, digital platforms are probably the best area for spreading out marketting message forwarded to youth segment. There are over 1 million users of social media networks in Latvia. Moreover country with rate of 55% occupies second place in Europe according to use of social media. Involvement is so high that even Latvian government uses social media as a communication tool with citizens.

Competitor's Analysis. Since the day company X entered Latvian market with brand Z, they were already dealing with genuine competition in there. Even though this brand was created copying successful brand Y phenomena in Lithuania, to develop brand awareness in Latvia was a lot harder.

Number of poor quality and low price goods provided by foreign trademarks especially for youth segment increased significantly in Latvia during last 3-5 years. (Brand for Baltic, 2010, 36psl) Even if theoretically it should not affect brand Z sales, as this brand is not considering low price and poor quality providers as their direct competitors, new giant entrant – H&M could not be ignored.

Hennes & Mauritz enetered Latvian market on 2013 and it is considered to be one of the harshest competitors in retail clothing industry as a whole. Even though the CEO of company X in the interview was assuring that H&M appearance will not make any negative impact on company's turnover, the competitive situation changed a lot. (Grinkevičius P., 2013). Even on social media platforms H&M is gathering big masses of fashion lovers. Today H&M facebook fan page counts 21.656.972 of followers. Moreover, even before this giant entered Latvian market, company RetailBaltics managed to create fan page called "Bring H&M to Latvia", which today counts to more than 2.700 followers. H&M strategy is to answer to millions of fans within couple of minutes as they share their ideas and opinions, moreover they used to link their platforms with third-party blog posts that provide wider range of information on fashion industry activities. Brand's engagement with its customers is really spectacular as posts on Facebook appear several times a day. Major brand Z competitor's activities on social media platforms are provided within a table below (See Table 1 for competitor's social media activities).

Table 1.

Competitor's analysis considering their social media networking activities

Company	Amount of followers	Social media platforms used	Average frequency of engagement	Most common content
H&M	21.656.972	Facebook (international)	Twice a day	Clothes combinations; Events promotion; Answers to followers questions; Contests; Customized content according to country.
	2 700	Facebook (Latvia)	2 times a week	Information on H&M activities; Surveys; Clothes combinations posted by followers
	~2.500.000	Google+ (International)	Updates on daily basis	The same information as on Facebook; Eye-catching imagery
	6 565	Twitter (International)	Several times a day	Responding to mentions (although response rate is relatively poor); Q&A campaign with David Beckham;

LPP S.A. **Reserved**	430	Draugiem.lv (Latvian)	Once a month	Links to official web page; New collections; Customer's reviews; Information on sales/promotions
	1.632.356	Facebook (International)	2 times a day	Information on events; New collections; Sales/discounts; Answers to followers problems, ideas; Motivational quotes.
	1060	Twitter	Several times a day	Pictures; Answers to mentions; Discussions
LPP S.A. **Mohito**	292	Draugiem.lv (Latvia)	Once a day	Discounts; Visual information;
	585.322	Facebook (International)	Twice a day	Discounts; Clothes combinations; Contests
	21 300	Instagram (International)	Once a day	Pictures of celebrities wearing brand's clothes; Discussions with followers behind pictures
AS Poldma **Kaubanduse** **Denim Dream**	4.239	Facebook (Latvia)	4 times a week	Links to online store; Contests that encourages to invite your friends to join the page; Local celebrities advertisement; Ads on discounts that are available only for 1 day;
	29	Twitter (Latvia)	Not active anymore	Links with bloggers;

Stockmann PLC Seppala	110.757	Facebook (International)	4 times a week	Discounts; Links to blogers pages that put ads of Seppala; Answers to customer's queries.
	347	Draugiem.lv	Twice a month	Surveys; Discounts; Clothing combinations
	135	Twitter (Latvia)	Not active anymore	Discounts;

Despite H&M entrance in Latvian market and social media spaces as well, brand Z is dealing with other strong competitors like AS Põldma Kaubanduse, Stockmann PLC, LPP S.A. Besides, it is important to mention that latvians are developing strong local textile and clothing industry too. As an example in Riga city there are 15 local origin chains of clothing and footwear, number is higher than in any other Lithuanian or Latvian region. (Brand for Baltic, 2012)

Strong competitor working in Latvian market is LPP S.A. which is working with well known brands for economy and youth segments like Mohito, Reserved, House, Cropp and Sinsay. Company's annual revenue on 2013 was EUR 10.45 million, though they are occupying just 5.22% of whole market share. (Consolidated annual report, 2013) The intensity of social media communication within LPP S.A. brands is provided on a Table above (See Table 1 for competitor's social media activities). While analyzing LPP S.A. performance on social media spaces, it was noticed that differently from retail giant H&M, LPP S.A. brands for youth have their fan pages on Latvia's local social media networking platform draugiem.lv.

Another internationally popular "multibrand" competitor is "Denim dream". The concept of this brand, which is owned by "AS Poldma Kaubanduse" is very similar to what brand Z offers to its customers. Their target is audience with higher income, as clothes provided in the stores are containing famous labels such as

18

Tommy Hilfiger, Calvin Klein, Tom Tailor and many others. As company is rapidly growing, they are investing more and more resources for media communication with customers. They had opened online store, which is available in three languages and despite of ability to order clothes online, they apply permission marketing techniques by allowing to subscribe promotional messages and get them directly to e-mail. More information about their activities on SNS is provided within Table above (See Table 1 for competitor's social media activities).

With a market share of 11.5% in Latvia, company Stockmann PLC operates within two market segments. "Lindex" stores are orientated more towards economic segment and families, while "Seppala" stores intend to attract similar market audience as brand Z. (Euromonitor International, 2014) "Seppala" stores provides wide assortment of goods with great balance between price and quality. Customer reviews prompt that customers appreciate wide assortment within stores and mostly are complaining about lack of sales and discounts. (Yell reviews, 2010). Although on social media networks, "Seppala" team gathers hundreds of thousands of followers and mostly discount ads are placed within their official Facebook fan page. For more detailed social media communication analysis of "Seppala" (See Table 1 for competitor's social media activities).

PESTEL Analysis. *Political.* The fact that Latvia joined EU on 1 May 2004, makes the idea of investing into this country even more attractive. Doing business in EU country is more secure as laws and regulations are applicable equally to all member countries. Therefore, business environment of local - Lithuanian market and Latvian one does not differ much, therefore in many cases company can centralize its activities and in this way save up a lot of money.

Moreover, with the score of 126, Latvia is most corrupted Baltic country (Transparency International, 2009). It can result in difficulties doing transparent business, especially while competing with other local companies for best store locations in the country.

Economical. According to Latvia's statistics, average monthly salary in Riga region (where brand Z stores are opened) is higher comparing to other Latvia's regions. 815 Eur per month was announced as average monthly salary in Riga city and its region on 2013. (Latvijas Statistika, 2014) It means that people getting average or higher income in Riga could be perceived as potential customers of brand Z.

Today Latvians have free market economy, what means everything is regulated by appropriate laws and commercial rights are well protected.

Comparing retail growth rate in Baltic States with other European regions, rate grows at a relatively high level. Within last year, 2014, retail trade (except motor vehicles) in Latvia grew at a rate of 4%, while average retail trade growth rate within European Union countries on 2014 was only 2%. (Interim Consolidated Financial Statements, September 30, 2014)

Social. First of all, language difference is very important indicator. As an example for Latvians, any Lithuanian brand name would not make any sense, therefore it would be more difficult to remember or distinguish. This may be a major reason why parallel brands orientated towards youth segment in Latvia and Lithuania were lauched upon different names.

Moreover, it is essential to consider that it is multi-lingual country and 37.5% of Latvia's residents are speaking only in Russian. (Juzefovics J., 2011) This factor should be strongly considered in order to improve customer's service. Employers should seek for employees speaking in both – Latvian and Russian languages in order to assure high quality service within company's stores. Latvians are very keen to preserve their cultural identity and language, so in terms of social media communication, the best bet is to speak to audience in their local language. (Cormack Consultancy, 2011)

20

While considering demographical characteristics of Latvian residents, statistics showed that on 2014, 54 141 of Riga's residents where counted to fit into age range of 25-29 and 50 450 people within age of 30-34. In summing up these two age groups, exact size of brand Z target audience in Riga is revealed. (Latvijas Statistika, 2014)

While overlooking media trends in Latvia, during the past several years, there was noticed a decline of public media audience, it may be a consequence of poor content quality and TV digitalization. (Rozukalne A., n.d.) At the same time decrease in traditional media usage increased popularity of social media networking and internet consumption. While analyzing social media patterns in Latvia, it was discovered that one of their most popular local social network platform today has more than 2.6million registered users, what considering Latvia's population is incredibly huge rate. Draugiem.lv gathers huge local community and is usually used for business purposes as well.

Most concentrated and most developed Latvian city is Riga. With the population of 658 640 it strongly outpaces other Latvian cities. It explains the reason why so far, company X expands only in Riga city.

Not less important indicator is aging population in Latvia. In the future it may have negative effect on revenues deriving from youth segment, which is one of key company's drivers now.

Technological. For the fact, Latvia has well developed infrastructure. For today, Riga city is the most relevant concentration point while we are talking about company's X activities. Additionaly to that, it is important to mention that Riga is a key hub of railway infrastructure. Moreover, this particular city has biggest airport in Baltic States.

Comparing Riga city with Vilnius, the supply of commercial space in Riga is 1.4 times greater and commercial space as well as is 1.6 times more expensive.

21

(Brand 4 Baltic, 2010) Therefore, for any company settling down in Riga, it is very important to assure that commercial space is used in the most efficient way.

Moreover, according to the 2013 trends of clothing purchasing online, Latvia was the last country among Baltic States, as only 15% of clothes were purchased online on 2013. This indicator may show that people tend to buy clothes more in store than online, what may count as an advantage for company X as they do not promote e-shops of their own brands at all. (Consumer barometer, 2013)

Environmental. The most important environmental aspect for clothing industry is climate in the country where business operates. Here Latvia brings huge advantage against for example southern European countries. Climate zone in here brings 4 very different seasons while each requires different kind of clothing, consequently people spend more in here comparing to people living in the Southern Europe.

Legal. Since the year of 2004, when Latvia joined EU, consumer rights protection in the country developed significantly. Therefore, it stimulated clothing retailers, including company X, to raise a bar assuring that all operations meet all the quality standards.

Another important legal factor is that Latvians have very strict advertising laws in a country, what makes marketing centralization process within a company more complicated. (Saeima, 1999)

SWOT analysis. In this part the whole situational analysis, considering internal brand Z situation and external factors, will be systemized by employing SWOT analysis (See Table 2 for summary of situational analysis provided in SWOT). Table 2.

Brand Z SWOT analysis

Strengths	Weaknesses
• Sells globally well know and appreciated brands;	• Brand Z ignores local Latvian social networks, such as Draugiem.lv while competitors

• Belongs to company X which has huge financial and human resources, therefore more money could be dedicated to communications and marketing; • Franchisee agreements with biggest luxury and youth brands that company X has, would allow to increase assortment within brand Z stores; • As company X is franchisor of Zara, which is perceived as social media networking queen with more than 23 million followers, this connection could be used for gathering audience on brand Z fan pages. • Good strategic locations of the stores; • Brand Z targets relatively huge market segment	are already engaging with their customers in there; • Poor management of social media networking as posts are updated approx 4 times a month; • Internet platforms capabilities not used properly; • Very slow brand expansion as during 9 years only 2 stores were opened. • Lots of money for brand Z advertising is invested into traditional media channels which popularity is decreasing at huge rates, not excluding Latvian market as well.
Opportunities • To employ social media communication in this way increasing brand involvement what at the end may result in increase of sales; • Collaboration with other company's X owned brands on social media platforms that targets the same target audience; • Overall living quality in Latvia increases year by year what would lead in bigger expenditure on branded clothing.	**Threats** • Competition with giant retailers such as H&M which occupies not only market shares but social media spaces as well; • Tendency of audience to switch towards markets, more customized boutiques or internet stores rather than choose stores on supermarkets; • Aging population trends in Latvia further could result in decrease of brand Z target audience • Because of high level of corruption in a country, it could be hard to maintain and develop

	transparent business.

Theoretical Aspects of the Problem. Published research on communication through social media and other digital channels has grown significantly in recent years as its power and importance for business is no longer debated. Social networks are used by more than 70% of internet population. (Waddington, S., 2012). Researchers found out that there are plenty of benefits that marketers claim to achieve through social media channels: increase exposure, increase traffic, develop loyal fan base, reduce marketing expenses, improve sales and many others. (Stelzner, 2013 May) Before starting brand's life within social media, company has to figure it out what content is most attractive and relevant for their target audience. Social media communication purpose can be: collaboration, education, communication or entertainment. (Safko, Brake, 2009, p.7) Accoridng to Scott, D. (2011) to decide on which social media platforms to enter should be very last decision. Social media is all about enabling conversations among your target audience. (Safko, Brake, 2009, p. 681) Company life within social media begins with fan base creation. While Facebook and Google offers ad campaigns with so called pay-per click advertising it can perfectly be used as one of the options to gather more target audience to company's social media page. (Sweeney, Craig, 2011, p.17) However this way is more useful for new companies, while for ones with reputed brand the buzz can be created by offering discount codes on pre-orders of the product. According to Tuten and Solomon (2013, p. 106) top three reasons why people share and spread content "socially" are because they find it interesting/entertaining, helpful to others or just to get laugh. When target audience is gathered, it is important to keep them entertained and involved. Equally essential is to schedule social media content for the months, weeks and individual days. Golden rule according to Augostino (2007, p.11) is to make updates once a week, it would make social media account "live", without being overbearing. Scott, D.(2011) in his book "The New Rules of

24

Marketing & PR" author emphasized that it is essential thing to participate within forums and actively use social media platforms by appearing on discussions with followers and answering them all the questions. Some recent studies found out that brand- centric communities often fail because they tend to focus more on company's needs than on needs of community. (Safko, Brake, 2009, p 684) In such communities people tend to divide in certain groups according to their type of behavior. Some community members tend to share experiences more than others, while biggest part of community members stick towards non-interactive behavior, such as just reading comments of others. According to Park and Cho (2012) one of the major reasons why people join social media communities is to learn about previous product experience. (Tsimonis G., Dimitriadis S., 2014, p. 330). According to social technographic ladder created by Forrester (Tuten, Solomon, 2013, p. 75) there are six types of people on social media: creators, conversationalists, critics, collectors, joiners, spectators and inactives. Type should be identified in order to apply social media communications tactics and to connect with company's intended customers. According to research made by Tsimonis, Dimitriadis (2014, p. 334) most important and interactive activities within social media are competitions with prizes and daily communication with users.

Empirical Research

This part is aimed to execute market research which will help to get deeper understanding of what factors affect target customers involvement in communication through social media. In this section quantitative research will be conducted and results will be analyzed applying methodical approach. Empirical research will consist of three parts: description of research methods, data collection process and interpretation of the results.

Aim and Objectives of the Research. Main purpose of empirical research is to figure it out what factors affects brand Z target audience involvement in communication through social media. The insights will be used in improving brand's communication techniques on social media spaces. Therefore, objectives of research comprise of:

- Identifying target market's overall social media involvement;

- Investigating major social media purpose: educational, entertainment, collaboration, communication (Safko, Brake, 2009, p.7)

- Identification of brand's target audience behavioral characteristics and preferences within social media platforms by revealing which type of users they are (creators, conversationalists, critics, collectors, joiners, spectators, inactives);

- Revealing target audience's engagement with fan pages and major brand Z competitors on social media spaces;

- Investigating most effective techniques and channels that would encourage target audience to actively participate in communication with brand Z on social media;

- Identifying target customers overall involvement with fashion;

- Ascertain respondent's current engagement with a brand on social media.

26

Theoretical Foundations of the research

In order to assure precision of each variable related with research question and observe the correlations between them, some theoretical models were used.

Social Media Involvement Model. One of the core variables of this research was overall social media involvement. The previous studies examined what factors make impact for intensity of social media use. According to Mantsumitrchai and Park & Chiu (2012) gender and age can be used in explaining factors which determine social networking systems adoption. (Choo-Hui Park & Yong June Kim, 2013, p.24) Moreover, customer's involvement into any process, product or brand, according to Bloch and Richins (1983) can be classified into three categories: personal, physical and situational (Zaichkowsky, 1985, p.342). Therefore while identifying factors that affects intensity of social media usage, the essence of these three involvement categories can be considered.

Personal involvement. According to hypothesis provided within Choo-Hui Park & Yong June Kim (2013) article, personal aspect affects involvement into social media platforms when individual feels that certain system could be useful for him. The perceived usefulness and value could vary, as one may benefit from provided ability to communicate with friends through social media platforms, while another may found it more useful for gathering information or expressing themselves.

Physical involvement. Zaichkowsky (1985) described it as characteristic of the object that may differ while interest increases. While analyzing aspects of social media physical involvement, trust and reliability of social media were considered as major factors that tend to positively affect usage of these systems. (Choo-Hui Park & Yong June Kim, 2013, p.25) If people find social networks trustworthy and secure, they probably will use it more intensively.

27

Situational involvement. It is a temporary increase of interest towards certain object. (Zaichkowsky, 1985) In social media it is all about revealing personal information on certain circumstances.

Social Technographic Ladder Model. The theory introduced by Forrester research, explaines types of people based on their interaction with social media. Therefore this model was employed in order to ascertain what factors affects customers involvement through social media with brand Z. (Tuten, T., & Solomon, M., 2013 p.76) Types were created based on activities that occur within social media spaces. Therefore, theorists admitted that some people may fit into several categories. Theory was used within a survey in order to better understand what activities attracts people the most, which social technographic type is dominant one and how it can be employed for better communication. Characteristics of each type are provided in a table below (See Table 3 for social technographical characteristics):

Table 3.

Social Technographic Ladder

Social Technographic Types	Characteristics
Creators	• Create content; • Add value to the site; • Contribute content to be shared.
Conversationalists	• Maintain duscussions.
Critics	• Reactors to the content rather than creators; • Do not create original content, but their contributions are highly valued within commnity.
Collectors	• Efficient users of social content; • They tend to follow and keep updated on information they want; • Help communities to which they belong by sorting and rating the content.
Joiners	• Maintain a profile on social networks, doing it for fun.
Spectators	• Consume content of others, while do not create or share content themselves.
Inactives	• Avoid social communities; • Are online but do not participate.

Note. From „Social media marketing"by Tuten, T., & Solomon, M., 2013.

Uses & Gratifications theory. This is very old theory explaining the tendencies of media usage. Moreover, theory provides insights about how media tools are adopted by mass audiences. As social media nowadays is booming and replacing the traditional media sources, many researchers were trying to adapt this theory for social media spaces. Therefore in answering the question what factors have impact on media usage tendencies and choices, U&G theory assumes that individuals tend to match media usage patterns with their goals. Basically, theory suggests that user seeks for media platform which allows him to fulfill his needs. Model of the theory is provided on a figure below (See Figure 1 for conceptual model of U&G). Further in the research, the major purposes of social media usage between brand Z target audience will be revealed.

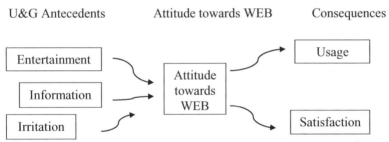

Figure 1. Conceptual model of uses and gratification. From „Uses and Gratifications Theory and E-Consumer Behaviors", Journal of Interactive Advertising, by Luo, X. (n.d.), p. 34-41

Starting from the beginning, U&G theory suggests that main goals which media consumers try to achieve are entertainment and education. (Luo, X. (n.d.), p.34-41) Last mentioned objective within a survey will clarify what form of information social media users found more useful and interesting. Do they prefer more user-generated content or do they prefer to have higher authority to control it. Do the opinion leaders make influence to them or it is more interesting to be involved into conversations with other fans rather than professionals of the industry. Respondents of the survey will be asked what kind of information is most relevant and how many fashion leaders are they following at the moment. While entertainment ascendant will be revealed by providing questions within a survey about contests in which respondents would be willing to participate in and ascertaining what other forms of activities would be entertaining for this particular audience. On the further research, based on Safko and Brake (2009) other two goals of social media consumption would be added: collaboration and communication.

Moving towards factors that according to conceptual model (See Figure 1 for model of U&G theory) formulate attitude towards Web and leads to its consumption, irritation factor has to be considered. This factor provides negative effect to usage of social media. Within a survey it is revealed by asking what post frequency in respondent's opinion is most optimal. Moreover, respondent's attitude towards interruption and permission marketing techniques will be ascertained, taking into account that some marketing tools which are used within social media spaces could be perceived as irritating and in this way reduce overall involvement with a page.

All these ascendants would formulate attitude towards WEB what consequently would increase or decrease usage and satisfaction of fan page. (Luo, X. (n.d.)

The final stage of theory is usage section, which indicates consequences. It includes means of social media that target group employ and frequency of the usage. As well as another consequence provided within this model is satisfaction, which in this particular case would result in satisfaction and involvement not only with social media, but with a brand as well.

Research methods

As there are no previous researches made on social media involvement with brand Z particularly, the empirical research was made by collecting primary data.

Quantitative research method was chosen due to several arguments:

1.   Wider range of respondents could be reached, considering time and geographical restrictions;

2.   Language barrier existence (as respondents are Latvian residents);

3.   Collected data could be easily interpreted in numerical terms in order to ascertain trends;

The purpose of the research was to get the insights about brand Z target group, their preferences and needs for social media communication. Data was collected by Solid Data Research Company for Baltic Countries. Final survey was provided in local Latvian internet platform VisiDati.lv. 205 respondents filled in the questionnaire during 7 work days, starting from November 11, 2014. Research was drawn up into Latvian language in order to assure representativeness of results. Survey was distributed to specific target audience for completion. Appropriate target respondents were people living in Riga city and in the regional areas and fitting to the age group of 25-34.

Research instrument

Questionnaire consists of 23 questions that will help to better understand what factors affect brand Z target customer's involvement in social media communication.

Research instrument which is provided in table below (See Table 4), was prepared by using some previously made academic research papers, which were constructed to reveal social media involvement, fashion involvement, motives to follow fan pages and involvement into blogging.

31

Table 4.

Research instrument framework

Aim of examination	Factors	Questions	Source
Demographic characteristics	Age, gender, income, place of living	1;23	Developed by author
Social media usage patterns	Frequency	2	
	SNS platforms used	3	
	Personal blogging involvement	4	Okdie, B. (2011)
	Blogging preferences	5	Developed by author
Social media involvement	Personal involvement	6 (from 1 to 4;9)	Choo-Hui Park & Yong June Kim (2013)
	Physical involvement	6 (5;6)	
	Situational involvement	6 (7;8)	
Customer's involvement with fan pages within social media platforms	Goals	7 (1;4)	Malciute J. (2012)
	Resources	7 (2)	
	Perceived cost/benefit	7 (3)	
	Amount of competitive fashion brand's followed on social media	20	Developed by author
Motives for social media usage	Learning about products, participation in contests, belonging to community, discounts, information gathering, involvement to decision making, customer service	8	Developed by author
	Motives for community feeling	12	Developed by author
	Stimulus for participation in contests	13	Developed by author
Marketing techniques	Interruption marketing (tools, frequency)	10 (4;5)	Developed by author
	Permission marketing (tools, frequency)	10 (1;2;3)	
Content relevance	Main message of the page	11	Developed by author
	Everyday message	16	
	Data presentation techniques	9	Developed by author
	Frequency of posts	15	Developed by author
Social technographics (6 types of people based on how they interact with social media	Creators	14a	Developed by author, but based on Tuten, T., & Solomon, M. (2013 p.76) analysis
	Conversationalists	14c	
	Critics	14b	
	Collectors	14d	
	Joiners	14e	
	Spectators	14e	
	Inactives	14f	
Fashion involvement	Product involvement	17(1)	Cass, A (n.d.)
	Purchase decision involvement	17(2;3)	
	Social approval motives	17(4;5)	
	Sensory pleasure motives	17(6)	
	Functional motives	17(7)	

	Fashion awareness	18	McFatter D. R.,2005
	Amount of opinion leaders followed	19	Developed by author
Involvement with brand Z on social media, evaluation of their facebook platform	Current involvement with brand Z facebook page, involving factors	21;22	Developed by author

Note. Full Questionnaire is provided on Appendix 3

Construct measuring social media involvement, which was based on theory of involvement and designed by Choo-Hui Park & Yong June Kim (2013), was slightly changed because previously made research was focused particularly on SNS involvement.However this research is focused not only on social networking, as it includes blogging practices and permission marketing teqniques as well. Therefore, considering time restrictions and topic amplitude, not all attributes were used. Leaving 5 statements to measure personal involvement 2 for psychical and 2 for situational.

Question 7 was included into research, as according to van Doorn et al. (2010) variables such as goals, resources and perceived cost/benefit of interaction with a brand in social media are expected to influence customer's engagement with brands. (Malciute J., 2012) Applying this construct for research, amount of statements was reduced leaving one for each variable, because of time restrictions. Moreover, construct was developed by author adding one more statement "I browse on social media fan pages because I am interested in the brands they are dedicated to" in order to better understand what is major goal of joining fan pages: belonging to community or interest in a brand itself.

Based on Cass, A. (n.d.) analysis, construct within question 17 was generated in order to measure motives for fashion clothing involvement. Determining factors such as materialism acquisition centrality, materialism posession defining success, materialism acquisition as the pursuit of happiness and self monitoring sensitivity

33

were excluded, as these attributes have been determined by original author as personality traits rather than motives for fashion clothing.

Additionally to question on fashion involvement, variable of fashion clothing awareness, which according to Tigert, Ring and King (1976) was part of five dimensions fashion involvement index, was reversed into the coding procedure and provided as question 18. (McFatter D. R.,2005)

Three types of measurement scales were used in a questionnaire:

- 5-point Likert scale was used while developing constructs within questions 5-8;10;12;16;17;22.

- 10-point Likert scale was employed in analysis of content relevance within social media platforms (Question 11)

- Nominal scale was used to define demographic characteristics, such as gender,age and while asking respondents if they are currently engaged with brand Z on social media, as well as in questions 1-4;9;13-15;18-21;23

By using reliable and valid scales, measurement error was controlled.

Research population and sample

Probability sampling technique was used within this particular research, because population was clear and defined. Random sampling method was employed, which assures that each member of population has equal possibility to fill in the survey and participate in the research. General characteristics of research population were determined to be residents of Riga city and regional areas (as brand Z stores are located only within this particular city), the ones that fit within age group of 25-34. Age range was defined by company X itself. Even though stores are orientated towards people having average and higher income, this factor was not taken into account while determining population. Such approach has been employed considering major aim of this research. Moreover, taking into account statistics, which states that women tend to be involved into fashion a lot more that man, representativeness of results was assured by distributing survey to target market that fits the requirements and additionally assure that 70% of respondents are females.

Sample was obtained by using discrete variables formula (Folz, D. H., 1996 p. 50):

$$n = \frac{z^2_{\alpha/2} \times [\pi \times (1-\pi)]}{\varepsilon^2};$$

Where n stands for sample size;

$z^2_{\alpha/2}$ = the standard normal distribution α-level critical value, which with 95% confidence level is equal to = 1,959

π = proportion of parameter in selective sample;

ε = sampling error, which is equal to 5%; $\varepsilon = 0,05$

From all the Latvian citizens 2 039 000, 34% are Riga and regional city area's residents, what is equal to 693 064. While from all people living in Riga and its region, targeted are only residents fitting within age group of 25-34 what based on Latvian statistics database is equal to 15% of total Riga population:

693 064 (15%) = 104 591

Therefore, proportion (π) from all Latvian population is counted as follows:

$$\frac{104\ 591}{693\ 064} \approx 0.151$$

Though sample size is equal to:

$$n = \frac{1.959^2\ (0.151(1-0.151))}{0.05^2} = \frac{3.838 \times 0.128}{0.0025} = 196.5 \approx 197$$

Data Analysis Methods

When all data was gathered, SPSS (Statistical Package for Social Science) program was used for further analysis.

As a preliminary assessment tool, descriptive statistics method was employed. Frequency of choices, demographical characteristics and percentage distributions of social media usage patterns were utilized for descriptive purposes. While in further analysis, correlations between variables were evaluated in order to assess experimental comparison.

In order to get deeper evaluation on how participant's preferences differ according social technographical types they belong to, independent sample t-test was employed.

Interpretation of independent sample t-test prompts that if the sig (2-tailed) value is less than or equal to 0.05, conclusion that there is statistically significant difference between two means could be made.

Spearman correlation method was adapted in order to examine statistical dependence between variables. The assumption of Spearman correlation states that values of both tested variables, increases or decreases at the same time and it is called monotonic relationship. Moreover, interpretation of method prompts that strength of correlation between variables is evaluated assuming that:

- .00 - .19 – correlation is very weak;
- .20 - .39 – weak;
- .40 - .59 – moderate;
- .60 - .79 – strong;
- .80 – 1.0 – very strong (Statstutor, n.d.)

Therefore this method was chosen to test relationships between dependent variables such as social media involvement and fashion involvement together with independent ones like:

- Involvement to fan pages;
- Most beneficial information on social media;
- Motives to join fan page;

- Preferences of information receiving;

- Motives for community feeling.

Other variables will be evaluated by finding most frequent answer or calculating and comparing means in order to systemize construct questions.

Validation of scales measurement. Before starting evaluation of results, The Cronbach's α coefficient tool was employed in order to check the reliability of questionnaire and degree of internal consistency in a survey. Commonly accepted rule while interpreting Cronbach's α coefficient is as follows:

$\alpha \geq 0.9$ – Excellent internal consistency;

$0.7 \leq \alpha < 0.9$ – Good;

$0.6 \leq \alpha < 0.7$ – Acceptable;

$0.5 \leq \alpha < 0.6$ – Poor;

$\alpha < 0.5$ – Unacceptable. (George, D., & Mallery, P., 2003)

Therefore, internal consistency was examined separately for every construct used within questionnaire (See Table 5 for internal consistency evaluation):

Table 5.

Cronbach's α coefficient and internal consistency of constructs within a survey

Variable	Questions	Number of Items	α coefficient	Internal consistency
Social media involvement	6	9	.689	Acceptable
Customer's engagement with fan pages	7	4	.886	Good
Fashion involvement	17	7	.881	Good

The constructs measuring customer's engagement with fan pages and fashion involvement have coefficients between .881 - .882 what shows good internal consistency. While internal consistency within construct measuring social media involvement was indicated only as acceptable. Although, summing up the results, test scores are solid and reliable enough for the further analysis.

Results of Analysis

Demographic characteristics. Total number of surveys collected was 205 (what is higher than calculated sample). Higher number of respondents participated in the research in order to assure representativeness of results, taking into account that some participants may claim not using social media at all. While answering question 2, 3 respondents out of 205 chose answer "I am not using social media at all" what means their responses could not be considered in further analysis. All in all, 143 women (~70%) and 62 (~30%) men filled in the survey. Bigger percentage of women was selected taking into account that according to O'Cass (2001), females have much stronger involvement in both: purchase decision and fashion involvement. Also compared to men, women are more likely to seek information on fashion. (Magie, A.,2008, p.55).

Geographical factor showed that 154 (75.1%) respondents were Riga residents, while 51 (24.9%) stated that they are living in Riga region (Pieriga), within 50km radius from the capital of Latvia.

Further results claimed that there is no extreme distribution regarding income. 73 respondents stated that their monthly income is ≥ 501 EUR and these respondents are assumed to be potential consumers of brand Z assortment. Moreover, respecting respondent's privacy, this question was generated as optional (with an option to refuse to answer). Results are provided in following figure (See Figure 2 for demographical characteristics):

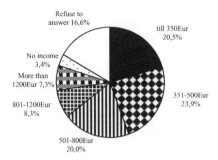

Figure 2. Demographical characteristics. Personal monthly income

Social media usage patterns. Moving on, in order to get picture about the patterns of social media usage within our target market, respondents were asked about average time they spent on social media per day and on the second question they had to name the platforms which they are already using for more than three months (See Figure 3 for social media usage frequency):

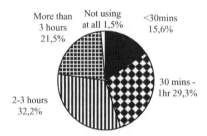

Figure 3. Social media usage patterns. Frequency

Distribution of social media usage frequency has been relatively equal. Survey revealed that respondents which are not very involved into social media activities and claimed to spend less than 30mins/day remains minority - 15,6%. All in all, results show that majority of target audience spends great portion of time on social media platforms every day.

Regarding social networking platforms used, as it was expected after situational analysis in Latvian market, most popular and useful social media network in Latvia is – Draugiem.lv, as majority 32,2% of respondents claimed using it for more than 3 months. Facebook platform not surprisingly is second most popular within this market, having 30,5% of our target market as users. Among other platforms mentioned, respondent's distribution was not extreme, but target market involvement into them is relatively low. Results of SNS platforms used are provided on the graph below (See Figure 4 for social media platforms used):

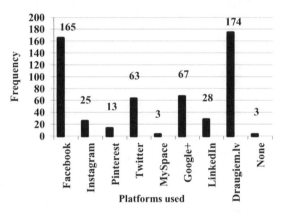

Figure 4. Social media usage patterns. SNS platforms used

As social media do not confine only to social networks, respondents involvement to overall social media activities were examined by asking about their blogging experience as well. Results showed that target audience's engagement with blogging is very unlike. Even though majority 97 (47,3%) said that they are familiar with „blog" concept, but they neither read nor write them, 78 participants (38%) claimed reading other people's blogs and 7.3% stated writing and reading blogs as well. What shows that roughly half of respondents are engaged and interested into that, while another half is not so much involved. Results are provided in a pie chart below (See Figure 5 for blogging involvement):

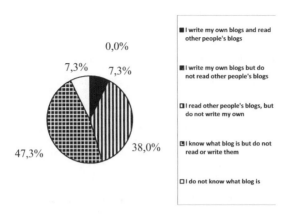

Figure 5. Personal blogging involvement

Before examining correlations between variables, descriptive statistics were employed. Table describing importance of factors which was assessed by calculating means of the variables and variability measures is provided in Appendixes. (See Appendix No 4 for descriptive statistics of variables)

Moving on the questionnaire, respondents were asked what manners to receive information are the most acceptable for them when it comes to social media. Output is provided within a figure below (See Figure 6 for means showing manners to receive information):

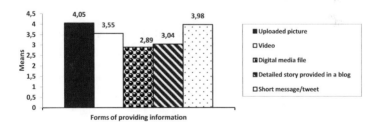

Figure 6. Means of manners to receive information on social media

Descriptive statistics revealed that the most acceptable way to receive information within social media platforms is in a form of pictures (mean 4,05). Therefore, by providing visualized information, target audience of brand Z could be engaged the most. While talking about other social media spheres (excluding social networks) visualized information could be employed by involving brand Z with Phlogging experience.

Social media involvement. Moving on with overall social media involvement measure and the construct composed by Choo-Hui Park & Yong June Kim (2013), descriptive statistics revealed that when it goes to social media, personal involvement and situational involvement are the dominant factors. Figure 7, demonstrates the means of 3 types of social media involvements. (See Figure 7 for means of social media involvement)

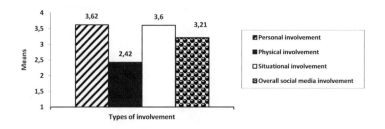

Figure 7. Means of social media involvement

Highest score of personal involvement suggested that usefulness and usage of social networking sites are the most important factors explaining intensity of social media usage. However, trust factor (physical involvement) as this research showed was evaluated at a lowest rate, what demonstrates that people not always feel safe and secure sharing their personal information on social networks. Low performance on physical involvement has to be taken into account, as it may reduce target audience involvement in social media activities related with a brand. This research confirmed the results of previously made analysis by Choo-Hui Park & Yong June

42

Kim (2013), where the same sequence of factors was revealed. To sum up, all these factors indicated overall social media involvement of brand Z target audience, which with a mean of 3,21 is evaluated as average.

Customer' engagement with fan pages on social media platforms.
Construct revealing participant's engagement with fan pages on social media platforms showed that target audience's of brand Z current involvement is relatively high, as a mean is equal to 3,06 (considering that mean of overall social media involvement of brand Z target audience was equal to 3,21). Results are provided within a figure below (See Figure 8 for means showing engagement to fan pages factors):

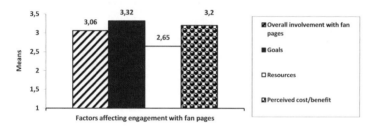

Figure 8. Means of factors affecting engagement with fan pages on social media

Results revealed that goals factor is determinant one (mean = 3,32).While there were two statements provided in ascertaining possible goals to join any fan page. First one was the interest to become a part of brand community (relational goal) and another one was interest to a brand that a page was dedicated to (consumption goal). Mean of last mentioned was equal to 3,23. Herewith, survey indicated that dominant stimuli to join any fan page, is goal to belong to brand community. The mean of this factor was equal to 3,4. (See Appendix No 4 for descriptive statistics) Therefore it was revealed that goal of browsing on social networking platforms effects the involvement to fan pages the most. Moreover, as respondents claimed willing to be part of brand community, it should be the major aim for a brand, to strengthen community feeling within social media.

While answering what factors according to brand Z target audience increase community feeling, most frequent answer was "ability to share problems/photos/questions within social media" (mean = 3,75). Results disclosing motives for community feeling are provided within a graph below (See Figure 9 for means showing motives for "community feeling"):

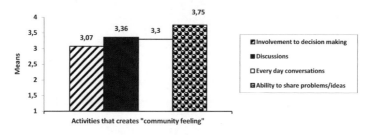

Figure 9. Means of motives for "community feeling"

Answers basically explain that the best way to create strong community within fan pages is to enable user-generated-content. Therefore by discussing on relevant topics, sharing the problems they face or ideas related with fashion, audience would create strong community ties itself.

Continuing with involvement to fan pages, respondents revealed fashion brands that they are currently following on social media. At the same time, harshest competitors of brand Z within social media spaces were highlighted. Results are provided within a graph below (See Figure 10 for involvement with fan pages):

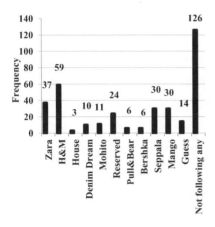

Figure 10. Fashion fan pages followed

Results shows that most frequently followed brands of our target audience are H&M (16.6%), Zara (10,4%), Seppala (8,4%) and Mango (8.4%). Considering that Zara and Mango are brands belonging to the same company as brand Z, revealed harshest competitors remains only Seppala and H&M.

Motives for social media usage. In order to identify the major purpose of social media communication, respondents were asked to reveal the factors that motivates them the most to follow any fan page. As it was found out during literature review, purposes can be: collaboration, education, communication or entertainment. (Safko, Brake, 2009, p.7) Figure 9 concludes all the answers (See Figure 11):

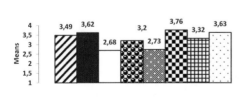

Figure 11. Means of activities that motivates to follow brand's fan page on social media platforms

Most dominant answers were discounts (mean = 3,76), learning about new products (mean= 3,63) and chance to participate in contests (mean= 3,62). By adapting Safko and Brake (2009) model, it was clear that respondents are mostly attached to educational and entertainment purposes.

As it was predicted before, participation in the contests was revealed as one of the strongest motives, therefore later within a survey respondents were asked in which contest they most likely would take place. Question was generated in order to discover what kind of contests are the most interactive for particular target audience of brand Z. 63 respondents (30,7%) stated that they would not participate on any contest within social media, while remaining 142 participants of a survey chose a certain contest to participate in. Results detecting respondent's willingness to participate in a contest within a social media are provided on a figure below. (See Figure 12 for contests types):

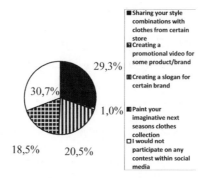

Figure 12. Types of contests that target audience would be willing to participate in

In summing up these results it is clear that majority of target audience would be willing to participate what means they belong to "creators" type, while others

46

could be interpreted as representatives of some other social technographic type. Further on the analysis, social technographic types of respondents will be revealed.

Social technographics. As it is very important to identify and understand our target audience within social media spaces, Forrester Research concept on social technographics was employed. (Tuten, T., & Solomon, M., 2013 p.76) In order to reveal types that our target audience belongs to and to ascertain what type is leading one , contest example of Pepsi was used. (Tuten, T., & Solomon, M., 2013 p.78). Results showed that vast majority of respondents (75 respondents), what counts to 36,6%, belongs to inactive users type, what means that these social media users are online but they tend to avoid social communities. While further results revealed that there are two other quite common types, so called joiners and spectators (42 respondents) what counts to 20,5% and critics – 43 participants (21%). This particular question was coded, therefore the meanings of each answer are provided within appendixes. When social media user's dominant behavioral types are revealed, company can apply certain tactics that fits the best for their audience. Results of social technographics are provided in a graph below (See Figure 13 for social technographics):

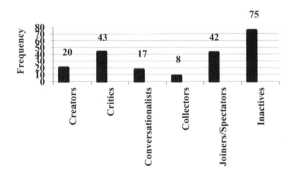

Figure 13. Social media types of interaction. Social technographics

Marketing techniques. Social media provides opportunity to employ permission marketing techniques, what means that customers can choose themselves if they want to get certain advertisements. Therefore marketing process in this way is more customize and usually brings better results. Within this survey the construct disclosing respondent's attitude towards permission and interruption marketing techniques was generated. Results of descriptive statistics, confirmed that permission marketing is way more acceptable (mean = 4,02), while interruption marketing was evaluated as annoying and usually ignored, as a mean of measurement statements was counted to 2,92. (For the descriptive statistics see Appendix No 4)

Content within social media. As descriptive statistics showed, one of the major motives for social media usage (mean = 3,62) is possibility to learn about new products, respondents were asked what tool works the best for them to lear. The results indicated that 92 respondents (44,9%) best learn about new products by collecting opinions of others about product/brand. It could be interpreted as a motive, explaining why people join fan pages as well. Distribution of results is provided in a chart below (See Figure 14 for learning tools):

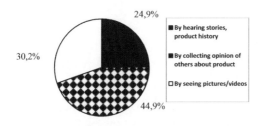

Figure 14. Tools preferred while learning about product/brand

Another very important aspect was to assess the content of message provided. As it was already determined in previous constructs, educational content is very

48

important within social media spaces. On further research, descriptive statistics revealed that most relevant information for respondents is information on discounts and sales. In a 10 point scale this statement had a mean of 7,59. Results prompt that any fan page has to be updated constantly in order to keep audience involved. All new collections and any discounts have to be provided within a page, as it would increase engagement and later may bring positive impact on sales as well.

As literature review revealed, the most interactive activity within social media was announced to be communication with users. Therefore question about daily communication within fan pages was designed. Respondents were asked what form of message would be most attractive if it would be posted daily. Statement "Message with a funny content" was evaluated the best (mean= 3,53), while the uncertainty about everyday message relevance, still remained relatively high. (For results of descriptive statistics see Appendix No 4)

Further on within a questionnaire respondents were asked, what in their opinion is optimal frequency for new post/tweet within any fan page. Distribution of the answers was pretty much equal, still the majority stick to the answer that the most optimal post frequency is 1-2 times/week (63 respondents (30,7%)). However, it is hard to make any assumptions so far, as second most frequent answer was – once a day (57 participants (27,8%)).

Fashion involvement. As overall fashion involvement was one of the most important factors to measure within this survey, construct was made up in parallel with previously made research on involvement to fashion clothing.

One more variable was added to this construct, showing overall fashion awareness of respondents. This measure was employed to show how important for target audience of brand Z is to be up to date with fashion trends and how this information would be valuable if provided within social media platforms.

49

IMPROVEMENT OF SOCIAL MEDIA COMMUNICATION

Descriptive statistics showed that overall fashion involvement is equal to the mean of 3,03. Dominant measure in a construct was functional motives, with a mean of 4,22, what is considered as very high evaluation. While second most important involvement factor was purchase decision involvement (mean = 3,27). Last mentioned prompts that respondents tend to think a lot before making purchase decision, therefore it could be perceived as a green light for social media communication as very often customer look for information on social media spaces before purchasing process. Results identifying means of factors are provided in a figure below. (See Figure 15 for means identifying fashion involvement)

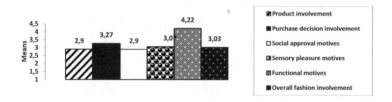

Figure 15. Means of factors identifying overall fashion involvement

While analyzing the results that ascertain respondent's awareness with fashion trends, it was observed that equal percentage of target audience 66 respondents (32.2%) is always up to date with fashion trends (but it does not necessarily mean that they could be switched to potential customers of brand Z), while equal amount of participants stated not being interested in fashion trends unless major change takes place. Results are provided within a pie chart below (See Figure 16 for fashion awareness):

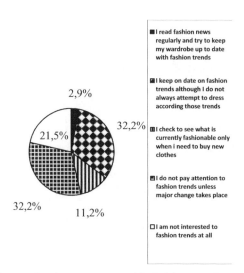

Figure 16. Respondent's awareness with fashion trends

Another variable measuring fashion involvement was examined by checking how many fashion opinion leaders, respondents are currently following. During literature analysis, Beaudoin, Moore, & Goldsmith (1998) stated that fashion leaders have influential effect on followers. Therefore question 19 was aimed to verify brand Z target audience's dependence on opinion leaders. Results demonstrated that 59% of respondents (121) are not currently following any opinion leaders, while 72 participants (35.1%) are following 1-5 fashion opinion leaders. Results of this particular question are provided within a pie chart below (See Figure 17 for opinion leaders followed):

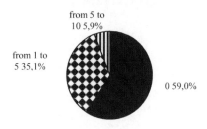

Figure 17. Opinion leaders followed

Involvement with brand Z. At the end of the survey respondent's involvement with brand Z particularly was examined. As it was expected vast majority of respondents stated not being engaged with this brand on social media spaces and not having intentions to do that (130 respondents (63,4%), what clearly shows that there is a huge need for improvement. Other 43 respondents (21%) claimed to be willing to join this page on social media. However, 3 respondents indicated being already engaged with brand Z on social media platforms, so they were diverted to another question and asked to evaluate brand Z facebook platform according to several factors. Results showing current engagement to social media page of brand Z are provided in a figure below (See Figure 18 for engagement with brand Z):

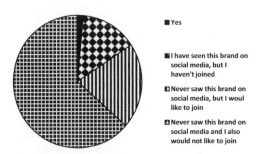

Figure 18. Current engagement with brand Z on social media

Although as the question was answered only by 3 respondents, responses could not be considered as reliable enough and this question was eliminated from the further analysis.

Factors importance in categories

Further on within a research, respondent's behavioral characteristics will be revealed distributing them into categories. Question 14 on a questionnaire helped to reveal social technographical types of target audience, dividing them into 6 categories: creators, conversationalists, critics, collectors, joiners/spectators and inactives. Results identified that majority of brand Z target audience (not considering inactive users) fall into critics and joiners/spectators types. Therefore, further research will examine if those two groups have statistically significant differences regarding motives and social media preferences. This would be helpful while providing managerial solutions, as by knowing who exactly our target audience is and how each type should be treated more customized tactics could be applied. Consequently, by knowing differences between groups, likelihood to connect with intended customers will be maximized.

Therefore, statistical signifance will be examined between dominant behavioral types: critics and joiners/ spectators. Hypotheses raised are:

H1: There are mean differences between "Critics" and "joiners/spectators" regarding their motives to join fan pages.

H2: There are mean differences between "Critics" and "joiners/spectators" regarding information they are interested to on fan pages.

T-test was employed in order to examine differences of means among variables and results are provided on appendixes section. (See Appendix 5 for test on statistically significant differences between critics and joiners/spectators)

Results revealed that there are no statistically significant difference between these two variables, therefore all previously made hypotheses were rejected. It prompts that there is no need to provide different kind of information or set different social media goals for these two groups.

Relationships between dependent variables and independent ones

After descriptive statistics were done, correlations will be checked among variables in order to find which ones are interrelated. Spearman correlation method was employed while testing relationships between social media involvement and fashion involvement together with: involvement to fan pages (Question 6), motives to join fan page (Question 8), most beneficial information within fan pages (Question 11), preferences on information receiving (Question 5) and motives for community feeling (Question 12).

In order to evaluate what correlation between variables exists, constructs measuring social media involvement and fashion involvement where transformed into new variables. All values of statements that show social media involvement or fashion involvement were summed up in this way simplifying further calculations (See Table 7 for results of correlation analysis):

Table 6.

Correlations between dependent variables and independent ones

Correlations

			SocialMediaInvolvement	FashionInvolvement
Spearman's rho	FanPagesInvolvement	Correlation Coefficient	,385**	,430**
		Sig. (2-tailed)	,000	,000
		N	205	205
	Uploaded picture	Correlation Coefficient	,366**	,217**
		Sig. (2-tailed)	,000	,002
		N	205	205
	Video	Correlation Coefficient	,323**	,106
		Sig. (2-tailed)	,000	,129
		N	205	205

Digital media file (audio)	Correlation Coefficient	,180**	,120
	Sig. (2-tailed)	,010	,086
	N	205	205
Detailed story provided in a blog	Correlation Coefficient	,256**	,186**
	Sig. (2-tailed)	,000	,008
	N	205	205
Short message/tweet	Correlation Coefficient	,148*	,190**
	Sig. (2-tailed)	,034	,006
	N	205	205
Motives Reviews	Correlation Coefficient	,383**	,316**
	Sig. (2-tailed)	,000	,000
	N	205	205
Motives contests	Correlation Coefficient	,348**	,209**
	Sig. (2-tailed)	,000	,003
	N	205	205
Motives community	Correlation Coefficient	,352**	,327**
	Sig. (2-tailed)	,000	,000
	N	205	205
Motives customer service	Correlation Coefficient	,372**	,360**
	Sig. (2-tailed)	,000	,000
	N	205	205
Motives submit ideas	Correlation Coefficient	,276**	,394**
	Sig. (2-tailed)	,000	,000
	N	205	205
Motives discounts	Correlation Coefficient	,347**	,286**
	Sig. (2-tailed)	,000	,000
	N	205	205
Motives Excl info	Correlation Coefficient	,290**	,350**
	Sig. (2-tailed)	,000	,000
	N	205	205
Motives learning	Correlation Coefficient	,395**	,323**
	Sig. (2-tailed)	,000	,000
	N	205	205
Information on sales and discounts	Correlation Coefficient	,426**	,313**
	Sig. (2-tailed)	,000	,000
	N	205	205
Experts ideas	Correlation Coefficient	,337**	,329**
	Sig. (2-tailed)	,000	,000
	N	205	205
new products	Correlation Coefficient	,429**	,378**
	Sig. (2-tailed)	,000	,000
	N	205	205
behind scenes	Correlation Coefficient	,340**	,416**
	Sig. (2-tailed)	,000	,000
	N	205	205
problems	Correlation Coefficient	,394**	,269**
	Sig. (2-tailed)	,000	,000

		N	205	205
involv decision making	Correlation Coefficient		,240**	,228**
	Sig. (2-tailed)		,001	,001
	N		205	205
Community motives discusions	Correlation Coefficient		,306**	,232**
	Sig. (2-tailed)		,000	,001
	N		205	205
Everyday conversations	Correlation Coefficient		,285**	,205**
	Sig. (2-tailed)		,000	,003
	N		205	205
Share problems	Correlation Coefficient		,337**	,418**
	Sig. (2-tailed)		,000	,000
	N		205	205

**. Correlation is significant at the 0.01 level (2-tailed).

*. Correlation is significant at the 0.05 level (2-tailed).

Social media involvement. Correlation between two dependent variables: fashion involvement and overall social media involvement was assumed to be statistically significant (r= +.255), although relationship is evaluated as "weak". (For correlation results between two dependent variables, See Appendix 6) Moreover "moderate" relationship was noticed between social media involvement and involvement to fan pages (r= +.506), what shows that people that are highly involved with social media, tend to be involved with fan pages on social media platforms as well. Moreover, it is important to mention that social media involvement relates with respondent's willingness to get information on sales and discounts (r= + .426) and information on new products (r = +.429) what is evaluated as "moderate" relationship among these variables. Mostly "weak" relationships were revealed while checking how social media involvement relates with independent variables of this research. Even though there were no coefficients showing strong correlations between other variables and social media involvement, all of them are assumed to be statisticaly significant. Moreover as all coefficients are positive, we could assume that as one variable increases, another one increase in value as well.

Fashion involvement. Results of other dependent variable relationships, did not show any "strong" correlations, although "moderate" relationships were noticed between fashion involvement and behind the scenes information (r=+. 416), what expectedly shows that as fashion involvement indicators increases, person's interest to exclusive information on fashion increases as well. Moreover, favorable relationship was found out between fashion involvement and involvement to fan pages, which was assumed to be "moderate" as r= +.430. Although assumption that asperson gets more fashion involved, more fan pages on social media spaces he is more likely to be engaged in. While another "moderate" correlation was identified between fashion involvement and importance of sharing problems, ideas with other page members, what is perceived as a motive to strengthen community feeling (r= +.418). Many other independent variables had statistically significant correlations with fashion involvement, although they were relatively weak.

Summary of empirical research analysis

During the research 205 respondents were surveyed, while only 202 of them were used for further analysis. Because of time and geographical limitations, results were collected by employing research company "Solid Data" and providing survey via internet platform.

Aims of empirical research where achieved, by portraying a picture of how target audience of brand Z use social media platforms, how much they are involved and for what purposes they tend to use it the most. Moreover behavioral characteristics and types of users were revealed. Analysis was made by employing descriptive statistics, ascertaining correlations between variables and looking for differences between behavioral types.

Summing up the results, statistically significant relationship was found between fashion involvement and social media involvement. Interpreting this result,

57

precondition that as person gets more involved with fashion, his social media involvement increases as well - could be made. For a brand, which is orientated towards fashionable youth it could be perceived as opportunity to gather fashion community around their brand by using social media spaces.

Moreover it was revealed that local Latvian social networking platform – Draugiem.lv is even more popular than Facebook, what means that in order to achieve very best outcome, both platforms has to be employed. Equally it is important to mention that social media does not confine with social networking only. Approximately half of participants claimed being interested in blogging, therefore an option to engage with blogging activites should be considered.

Moving on, survey detected that target audience of brand Z is mostly engaged in educational and entertaining activities within social media. As huge importance for educational information was revealed, later on analysis showed that there is a "moderate" statistical dependence between fashion involvement and interest in "behind the scenes" information. It means that by providing this information on brand Z social media page, there is a possibility that more fashion involved people will be attracted.

The dominant behavioral types were identified to be critics and joiners/spectators. As there were no statistical significant differences found between these two, there is no need to provide different kind of information in order to involve both behavioral types.

Moreover, as it was predicted, major competitor on social media spaces for brand Z is H&M. As second most commonly followed fashion fan page is Zara, which belongs to the same company X, brand Z could replicate some successful strategies used by globally popular fashion giant.

Data gathered from empirical research, will be used for creating social media communication plan for 2015.

Managerial Solutions

In general, all indicators prove relatively poor current performance of brand Z within social media spaces. So far there is only one social media network – Facebook, employed for communication purposes. Moreover, as respondents were asked during the research, if they are already engaged with this particular brand on social media platforms or would they intend to do that, results revealed quite negative target audience's attitude. It means that brand image has to be improved and stronger ties with current and potential customers have to be created by employing social media communication tools. Moreover while overlooking company's situational analysis it was revealed that digital marketing and e-commerce is the weakest and at the same time most promising marketing communications mix piece for brand Z.

Further on, managerial solutions for improvement of communication plan within social media spaces will be provided. Schedule for communications on social media platforms will be developed for 2015 year.

The proposed solutions would not change brand's image itself or current strategy drastically. Moreover communication plan would not require huge financial investments or other resources that would not be possible considering current position of company X and their annual marketing budget. What is more, communication plan will be based on social media success plan model provided by Brown, E. (2012, p.16-39). Book prompts that there are two major stages in communication plan creation: good strategy generation and implementation plan/budgeting. Although before starting plan development, major goals to achieve were raised invoking S.M.A.R.T. principle.

Goals

First of all the goals has to be set, in order to ascertain the outcome that is intended to be achieved by social media communication plan generated for brand Z.

Therefore George T. Doran's framework for management goals and objectives setting will be employed. Major goals of social media communication plan improvement are: 1) Increase brand Z awareness through social media platforms by building fan base. 2) Increase target audience's involvement with a brand Z on social media platforms by engaging with followers and providing relevant and attractive content;

First of all it is important to get attention and awareness. As framework promts, goal has to be *Specific*: 1) To reach approximately 300-400 views on each blog post. Brown E. (2012, p.21) estimated it to be achievable number during one year. *Measurable:* 1) Google Analytics is a free tool providing detailed information not only on amount of visitors in the blog, but as well to track total pageviews in a visit (Sauer, J., 2013, September 23); *Attainable:* 1) First of all current customers will be informed about brand Z blogging activites through e-mails and later on, potential audience will be gathered through contests, cross-promotions with partners or collaboration with other bloggers. *Relevant:* 1) To generate traffic within a blog is important, as it encourages more active discussions, it stimulates word of mouth about a brand and its products and therefore it can positively influence target audience's purchasing decisions. *Time bound:* 1) During one year (2015).

Another goal is orientated towards fan base creation on social networking platforms. Applying S.M.A.R.T. principle, this goal would be phrased as *Specific*: 2) To gather 10 000 followers within brand's fan page on Facebook. Number is realistic as it was already proved by example of parallel brand to brand Z on Facebook page. *Measurable:* 2) Number of fan reach can be tracked within Facebook page statistics interface in "Lifetime post reach by people who like your page" section. (Ernoult, E., 2013, March 18) Fan reach is more reliable measure than estimation based on number of followers/fans. Reasoning is simple, fan reach metric indicates appeal of content provided to your audience, while number of followers which are visible for everybody on every Facebook fan page includes the ones who may be hiding your posts from their news feed, so they do not really count as actual followers. *Attainable: 2)* Brand Z Facebook page already has more than 1000 followers. Moreover, fan base can be collected by generating contests that would encourage to "share"; applying cross-channel communication; collaborating with other company's brands on Facebook pages. *Relevant:* Content provided will not have sense and expected effect if there will not be content cosnumers. It is important for inducing discussions, sharing and active participation in contests. *Time bound:* 2) During year of 2015.

Although it was considered that not all social networking platforms have possibility to see "fan reach" number. *Specific: 3)* 3 000 followers on Draugiem.lv platform. Number on followers was estimated according to competitive brands performance on Draugiem.lv platform *Measurable: 3)* It can be tracked on front page *Attainable:* It is dominating platform among brand Z target audience; information provided in there will be specific in this way expecting word-of-mouth; current customers of brand Z will be informed through e-mails about activities in this platform*3) Relevant: 3)* Relatively big fan base is necessary for discussions, survey collections, interactive contests; *Time bound:* 3) During year of 2015.

Therefore it is aimed not only to gather huge fan base, but also to involve followers with conversations and activities within fan pages and blog. Follower's engagement is measured by amount of people who clicked anywhere on the post. This factor may not be that reliable as audience's engagement differs a lot on a content provided. Another solution is to use estimation of page success tools, and one of the most popular is Klout tool which puts all determining success factors into one algorithm. Although it is best suitable for Facebook or Twitter so far. Goal measuring follower's engagement is phrased as: *Specific: 4)* Reach Klout score of 60. *Measurable: 4)* It is a free tool, that recalculates score of the page several times a day

IMPROVEMENT OF SOCIAL MEDIA COMMUNICATION

Attainable: 4) Average Klout Score is equal to 40, but providing content that is valuable for followers, engaging with them regularly and investing some money to build a fan base, it is possible to reach 60 during one year. (Banfield, J., 2013, October 28) *Relevant: 4)* This score shows how influential your pages on social media spaces are, so the higher the number gets, the more involving your content is. Basically this measurement gives indication of how many people are giving attention to content provided. (Banfield, J., 2013, October 28); *Time bound:* 4) During year of 2015.

Strategical and tactical decisions

One of the most essential and primary steps before engaging with customers is preparation of the overall strategy. During this stage it is important to ascertain several things:

- Characteristics of target audience;
- Places where audience could be reached and informed about brand's page;
- Decision on social media platforms to enter;
- Intensity of communication;
- Page content development;

Strategy on defining target audience. Characteristics of target audience in this place do not confine on demographical characteristics of a potential customer. Before engaging with social media spaces it is equally important to reveal social technographic types of users, what would let us reveal page's online advocates and key connectors.

By summing up all findings it was revealed that majority of target audience falls into critics and joiners/spectators categories. However it was ascertained that these two groups do not differ regarding preferences of information provided. It is still important to consider "creators" as they are the most active layer of social technographical ladder.

Strategy on audience attraction. It is obvious that even an outstanding page without followers and participants is worthless. Therefore second step after target audience is defined, would be to develop a strategy on how to reach that audience. It is important to reveal the most dynamic places where relevant audience is usually gathering and to identify major influencers that would induce our target users to join brand's fan page. Therefore here are some tactics provided that would help to collect relevant audience faster:

1.   First of all current databases has to be used. As it was revealed during situational analysis, one of the permission marketing techniques that company X currently practice is collection of post-purchase customer surveys, which states that customer is willing to get promotional information through his email. In this way all current customers can be reached and invited to join fan pages on social media platforms what would enable more qualitative communication. Moreover, empirical research proved that permission marketing for target audience of brand Z is way more acceptable than interruption marketing methods.

2.   Later on, while sending promotional messages to current customers, links to social media communication platforms could be attached as an auto-signature together with every letter.

3.   Commenting on other blogs where fashion lovers communities are gathering, it would grab audience's attention and will lead viewers of other blogs to visit blog of our brand. Moreover during research it was revealed that majority of target audience is always up to date with newest fashion trends. Therefore it prompts that local fashion bloggers, which usually share

information on latest trends on their sites, could be relatively influential tie with target listeners of brand Z. Therefore it was examined that most popular Latvian fashion bloggers today are Agnese Kleina and Karina De Jesus. Summing up all the findings, optimal strategy would be first of all to actively participate within discussions on those blogs under the brand name and deliberate upon opportunity to collaborate with those bloggers. As both of the bloggers falls into target segment of brand Z and on their blogs they often tend to share and discuss on their personal outfit decisions, the opportunity to make barter agreement could be discussed. Brand Z could impose gift cards worth 200Eur for each blogger, so they could choose outfit from brand stores and later promote it on their blogs with a links to brand Z social media accounts provided. Barter agreements with bloggers could be made twice a year, on beginning of every fashion season, therefore it could be good advertisement campaign of new collection as well.

     4.   Another way to attract the audience was derived as a consequence of involvement type revealed during the research. It was identified that social media involvement of this particular target audience, depends a lot on situational factor. According to Zaichkowsky (1985) it proves that interest of the audience tend to increase just temporary depending on certain situation. Even though theory suggests that involvement is temporary, once you have huge amount of people following your page it is a lot easier to grab their attention and create a buzz. Social media advisers prompt that one of the most effective ways to build huge fan base is to employ so called cross-channel strategy. (Indvik L., 2011) Therefore this strategy could be applied for brand Z particularly as despite of decreased popularity of traditional marketing methods, company Z still invests big portion of money into traditional media campaigns. Consequently those findings where summed up to the solution of releasing an ad on local magazine that would encourage viewers to sign in to brand Z

Facebook or Draugiem.Lv fan page and withdraw branded souvenir from any brand Z store. Cross – channel strategy like this was used several times before, by brands like "Covergirl" and "Oscar de la Renta" while in both cases, amount of Facebook followers during the first day of campaign jumped up in a number of more than 5000. As brand Z is already promoting their collections on local Latvian Privata Dzive and Ieva LV magazines, the solution to place an ad in Privata Dzive magazine was made considering good ratio between relevant audience reached and cost. With magazine circulation of 46 600 and cost/full page of 1260Eur this was perceived as more suitable option than Ieva LV. As the ad is planned to be ¼ of the page, approximate price should be 315Eur. Another advantage achieved in particular brand Z case is that promotional campaign would encourage target segment not only to engage with fan pages on social media, but to get off the computer and visit stores as well.

     5.   Most social networking platforms allows for fan page moderator to show up what other fan pages he is currently following. As an example on Latvian networking site Dragiem.lv there is section called "partners" revealing connections that company/brand maintains. This may be perceived as another promotion strategy which provides opportunity to be visible on other related content fan pages and to reach target audience with minimum efforts and costs. Company X has huge competitive advantage as it is working with globally well known brands such as Zara, Tommy Hilfiger or Mango. Considering the fact that on Facebook platform neither of these brands has specific account created for Latvian market yet, Draugiem.lv network will be used.

     6.   It is planed that for the first two months audience's attraction will be dedicated only on marketers and communicators efforts, while before the

beginning of March (because it will be a beginning of new fashion season as well) the campaigns and contests will be employed expecting to encourage current followers to invite their friends and promote the page by sharing.The major aim is to make audience grow organically on its own. Although this opportunity would be available not in all of the platforms. As sharing activity is not valid on local Latvian site Draugiem.lv.

It is a common mistake that most businesses do while engaging with social media, as they expect huge masses of followers and communicators very suddenly, while in real life audience grows gradually. Even if at the very beginning company chooses to invest in advertisements on AdWords or Facebook what in most cases is very promising strategy, usually it takes more time to convert followers to communicators.

Strategy on social media platforms to enter. According to Willey (2012) to decide on which social media platforms to enter should be very last decision. Therefore in this particular case it is necessary to do it before generating strategy on content, as platform capabilities has to be considered before planning every message. Moreover, during literature review, interesting fact was found about social media preferences within Latvian market. It was identified that differently from social media preferences in Lithuania or Estonia, Latvians have their local social networking website, which today counts for more than 2.6 million registered users and so far is third most visited website in Latvia (after Google.com and Google.lv). (Cormack Consultancy, 2011) This is exactly what empirical research results proved. It prompts that many international businesses while entering Latvian market and communicating their brand on social media goes for traditional and globally popular platforms like Facebook or Twitter. While in Latvian market Facebook is only at #5 place and Twitter only #16. Therefore important lesson to learn is do not ignore opportunities that local social media offers.

Therefore, it was decided to work on developing both platforms: Facebook and Draugiem.lv.

Although social media is not limited to social networks only so in order to generate trustworthy and engaging social media communication, other options has to be considered as well. As 45,3% of brand's target audience claimed to be reading blogs and 41% stated to be currently following at least one fashion opinion leader on social media spaces it indicates that audience is willing to read blogs and have an opinion leader to follow. The most reccomended recommended point to start blogging journey is on website blogger.com which provides opportunity to create blog for free and link the account with Google+ platform, what will make fan base creation process faster.

Strategy on intensity of interaction. There is very tiny line between information on social media being involving to annoying. Herewith, it requires deep analysis and understanding of audience in order to find a right timing and frequency of providing a content. Brown, E. (2012, p.17) suggests that moderators of fan pages have to maintain a regular pattern in communications. Golden rule according to Augostino (2007, p.11) is to make updates once a week, it would make social media account "live", without being overbearing.

In order to verify or deny previously made researches, respondents during the survey where asked what in their opinion is optimal frequency of a new post/tweet. Results detected that distribution between answer "1-2 times a week" and "once a day" was pretty much equal. Therefore, before making a decision on strategy that should be adapted, observation of most successful and most intensively followed fashion fan pages on social networking platforms was made.

Taking ZARA as example of outstanding and effective marketing campaigns within social media spaces, observation was made by following their actions within

67

Facebook page. ZARA started social media era on 2002, and today their performance is outstanding. Frequency of updates within this platform is on average 3 posts a week.

Moreover it is important to consider negative antecedent that was presented together with U&G theory – irritation. In order to avoid this factor which may result in decrease of page usage and satisfaction, the solution to update posts within social networking platforms 1-2 times a week, was made.

Deciding on post frequency within blog, Brown E. (2012, p. 20) suggests to orientate towards 100 blog posts a year, what would be appropriate number in order to create and maintain certain audience viewing and commenting on a blog. It would result to approximately 2-3 posts a week. Frequency of new blog update should be planned considering that more gripping and encouraging news within fashion business are available before every new fashion season. Consequently, as more information at that time would be available to share, frequency of blogging should systematically increase.

Strategy on content development. The first goal is to set up a content that would be valuable for readers. Most of businesses especially the ones that operates within fashion industry, makes a major mistake by overcrowding their social media pages with hundreds of posts containing sales, offers or presenting new collections of clothes. This is exactly the content you expect to see on every clothing retailer's Facebook page. While Augostino (2007, p.11) is explaining that more effective way to grab customer's attention is by concentrating on qualitative and unique content of message. The lesson is simple – overdoing social media networking will turn off potential consumers instead of attracting new ones.

During empirical research U&G theory antecedents, prompting that entertainment and educational aspects of social media page/site leads to its usage and overall satisfaction, were revealed. Majority of respondents claimed that biggest motivators to join any fan page are contests, information on discounts and ability to learn about new products. The solutions for entertaining and educational content are provided in a table below. (See Table 7 for content on considering platforms capabilities and reasoning):

Table 7.

Content regarding platforms with reasoning provided for each

Platform	Content	Reasoning
Facebook	*Entertainment.* Pictures with 2 different combinations of clothing styles (with clothes from brand Z stores) asking to judge and pick the better one.	Orientation to critics, who want to be judges of content and express their opinion. It was revealed that audience learn about new products the best from opinions of others.
	Entertainment. Contest called "Clothes challenge" encouraging followers to share most original ways of wearing/ adjusting clothes bought within brand Z stores. Winner is selected according to amount of "likes" and will be awarded with a gift card of company's net stores.	Strongest fashion involvement motive was revealed to be – functional, what means that customers are ready to pay for quality of product and variety of functions performed; Contests – second biggest motivator to join fan page; Orientated towards critics and creators.
	Informational. Behind the scenes information and sneak-peaks from fashion shows and new collections of brands that are usually sold in brand Z stores as well (Diesel, Miss Sixty, Fornarina) Providing short videos from fashion shows or backstage pictures presenting new season campaigns. Share a content that is not available anywhere else	Fashion involvement has positive correlation with behind the scenes information; As information which is beneficial for fashion involved people is provided, it is important to consider that there was a positive correlation between fashion involvement and involvement to fan pages revealed.
Draugiem.lv	*Entertainment* Start the discussion on follower's everyday style encouraging them to share pictures of what they wear or what kind of style they like. During this discussion, brand Z persona would participate as well embodying role of the expert. On further stages expert role could be taken by local celebrities or influential local fashion bloggers.	During research respondents revealed their concerns about social media being insecure and unsafe, therefore this platform was picked for more personal engagement because in order to register to this local platform you need insider invitation; Orientated to critics and creators types; It was identified during empirical research that factor increasing community feeling the most, is ability to share ideas, thoughts and problems. Brand pages on Draugiem.lv platform is mostly dedicated for

		discussions
	Informative Providing a survey, with an intention to receive a feedback on assortment sold within brand Z stores	Benefit for company; This platform provides opportunities for surveys; It can be used while organizing further activities on a page
	Informative Promoting that it is a platform where discounts are announced first.	Providing reason to follow; During research biggest motive to follow fan page was revealed to be information on discounts;
	Informative Make FAQ alive and respond quickly	Motive strengthening community feeling the most – ability to share problems/ideas; Increase brand image and trust.
Blog	*Informative and entertaining* Section called "Celebrity look with brand Z. Providing outfit of locally/ internationally influential celebrity together with similar combination or style of clothing that is currently available in brand Z stores.	Survey revealed that most appropriate way to receive information is the one provided in picture format, what would result in Phlogging rather than Blogging. Would encourage buying; Youth target audience is more easily affected by celebrity phenomenon; Research revealed that majority of audience is willing to be up to date with fashion trends
	Informative Providing stories of famous brands that are sold within Brand Z stores.	Would be encouraging for fashion involved people;
	Entertainment Announce contest encouraging to create and rhyme a slogan about summer with brand Z, and to place it in the comments section. Winner will be awarded with gift cards worth of 100Eur to shop in brand Z stores.	During the research "create a slogan" contest was revealed as second most attractive one; One of the most famous Latvian blogger Agnese Kleina organized contest of similar concept on her blog before Christmas, which was linked with H&M and attained around 50 participants.

First of all the capabilities of platforms used has to be considered.

Despite of various kinds of information provided within fan pages, one of the key activities leading to success is moderator's participation in the discussions that appears on a page. As empirical research revealed, discussions is a second strongest factor building community within fan pages.

Implementation plan

When the strategy is generated next step is to put everything into the timescale and to calculate preliminary budget needed for plan implementation.

Equally important is to dedicate a person that would be suitable the best for this responsibility. Major work is not to set up the accounts, but to make them live. It takes lots of time and efforts in order to continuously communicate with audience, find out what they need and answer to their queries. So it is clear that strategy, which company X was employing before, will not work. So far, responsible person for social media communication of brand Z was stores administrator, who is aware with the message that brand Z wants to transmit, as well as has knowledge on fashion trends and goods provided within the stores. Most importantly this is a person familiar with a local language and culture. Although major problem in here was that current social media communicator clearly did not have any professional experience related with social media platforms and content management. Therefore as company X empowers marketing agencies to set up traditional marketing activities, social media communication specialists should not be an exception as well. Major aspects while considering good advisor for social media communication according to Brown E. (2012 p.18) are first of all to make sure the advisor is not advocate of only one popular solution such as for example only Facebook communication. Another advice is to measure experience in this niche by amount of time he/she spent on social media. And third very important aspect to consider is that voice, personality and manners of the person, which is responsible for company's social media communication, will be perceived as brand persona by target audience. This is why the most appropriate solution is to employ social media management specialist that could work in collaboration with brand's representatives. In this way company would assure that content is set up, distributed and managed by industry professionals. It was decided

71

to hire local Latvian specialists, therefore Cormack Consultancy was picked as the best option for price and value ratio. For the first year it was decided to take "premium" package, which will include features such as active building of audience and content creation as well. Price for this kind of service will range from 570Eur/month. (Cormack Consultancy.,(n.d.))

When instruments for communication plan are discovered, next stage is to provide timescale and prepare financial outline for those activities to happen. Considering all limitations, only approximate numbers will be provided, although current company's budgeting will be taken into account. Consolidated company's report (Consolidated annual report, 2013, p.24) reveals that for all company's marketing activities approximately 1 642 898 EUR are dedicated on annual basis. Considering that company works with 33 brands, we would assume that more or less the same amount of money to each brand's advertising and communications are allocated, what would result to 49 784 EUR per brand. This number would be assumed as brand Z annual marketing budget. Statistically on 2013 an average amount that businesses dedicated to digital marketing purposes was 35% of their marketing budgeting. (McCleary, J., 2014, June 6) Therefore preliminary budgeting for one year social media communication plan would count to 17 424 Eur. In the following table all activities are presented graphically, considering that they would be implemented from the beginning of 2015 (See Table 8 for Timescale and budgeting plan of social media communication activities):

IMPROVEMENT OF SOCIAL MEDIA COMMUNICATION

Table 8.

Implementation plan with timescale and budgeting

Social media communication instruments \ year divided into months and fashion seasons	2015												Budget (Eur)
	Spring/Summer							Autumn/winter					
	Jan	Feb	March	Apr	May	June	July	Aug	Sept	Oct	Nov	Dec	
Human resources													
Social media management specialists													570Eur/month = 6840Eur
Audience attraction													
Current customer's attraction to fan pages within social media through e-mails													0
Attaching links of social media fan pages with letters													0
Promotion on other company's fan pages													0
Audience growing itself (contests engaging to share)													
Barter agreement with influencial bloggers									Beginning of month				800Eur
Cross channel strategy (ad on "Privata Dzive" magazine)		End of month											315Eur
Facebook													

IMPROVEMENT OF SOCIAL MEDIA COMMUNICATION

Activity	Schedule / Notes		Cost
Contest brand Z clothes challenge			100Eur
Clothes combinations "wars"	Once a week - ~4 times/month		0
Behind the scenes (sneak-peaks from fashion shows and backstage pictures from promotional campaigns)	Diesel (February 12-19)*	Fornarina, Miss Sixty (New collection campaign) 25-30 of Aug	2000Eur
Draugiem.lv			
Discussions on everyday style with expert advisor	Encourage to engage with discussions every month presenting new expert which will be commenting on looks (Once a month)		~1200Eur**
FAQ section	Respond to customers queries as soon as possible		0
Surveys	One survey/quarter		0
Exclusive discounts for followers	End of season		0
Blogs			
"Celebrity look" section	Once a week - ~4 times/month		0
History of brands that company works with	1-2 stories a week - ~4- 8 stories/month		0
Contest on creating slogan "Summer with brand Z"	Beginning of month		100Eur
			Total: 355

*New York Mercedes-Benz Fashion week (n/d); **DIESEL BLACK GOLD (VIP OFF-SITE SHOW): $1,650 per person;

**Imposing 100Eur for expert every month

Total budget, including participation in fashion shows (what in most cases is sponsored by a company and does not count as marketing department expense) and cross-channel media marketing is equal to 11 575Eur, what counts to 23% of overall annual marketing budget of brand Z.

Conclusions

1. During situational analysis part it was revealed that brand Z considering company's X current resources and position on Latvian market has huge opportunities to grow and expand. Company invests great portion of resources to traditional marketing solutions, therefore while considering target market of brand Z, growing internet and social platforms popularity in Latvia, it is equally important to engage with social media activities as well. Moreover, major competitors of brand Z are already one step further. As an example Denim Dream today counts 4 239 followers on their Latvian Facebook page, Mohito – 585 322 while brand Z remains with 1140 followers on Facebook and is not engaged with any other social networking platform.

2. It was ascertained that target audience of brand Z is mostly engaged with educational and entertaining content on brand pages. Therefore it was suggested to generate contests that would encourage followers to share – create a slogan upon brand Z summer collection or share with ideas to use brand Z clothes in the most original way. As for educational activities it was decided to share stories on history and development of the brand Z or discuss on celebrity looks together with a team of experts.

3. Deeper analysis of current situation helped to investigate the opportunity of cross-channel communication for faster social media communication expansion. Data from collected customer surveys in stores can be used for informing current customers about social media activities through emails, while brand Z ads on magazines can include links of fan pages on social networks as well. Alike information on brand's public relation activities could be placed and shared within blogs or other social network platforms in this way increasing engagement with the event and quality of brand's social media communication.

4.   One of the most important findings assuming competitors analysis and results of empirical research was that so far brand Z was putting all efforts towards Facebook platform development, while most active social network site in Latvia – Draugiem.lv, which gathers a lot more target audience than Facebook. Therefore in order to get the best outcome from social media communication brand Z has to assure their presence in this platform on the first place.

5.   Empirical research was conducted in order to reveal which social technographical types are dominant among brand Z audience. It was identified biggest part of audience falls into critics and joiners/spectators social technographic types. During further research it was revealed that there are no statistically significant differences between these two types regarding content consumed or preferences on information within social media spaces. Assumption, that these two dominating types can be treated in the same way was made.

6.   As it was revealed that target audience's fashion involvement is relatively high and it correlates positively with overall involvement to social media, it was concluded that exclusive information on fashion trends, as an example, behind the scenes information from fashion shows has to be provided on fan pages. Approximate cost of providing behind the scenes information from fashion weeks was assumed to be 2000Eur.

7.   Research that was conducted prompted that for target audience of brand Z biggest motive to join any fan page is willingness to become part of the community. Therefore all activities on social media spaces has to encourage user-generated content, provide sections where followers can discuss, share their ideas and problems. Most importantly in order to not repeat one of the biggest competitor's on social media spaces – H&M mistakes, it is

77

crucial for brand to be there, to engage with customers and to provide experts opinion when needed.

8.   Considering all findings it was decided to employ social media management specialists in order to assure qualitative administration of social media activities. For the first year three most suitable social media platforms were picked to enter: Facebook, Draugiem.lv and Blogs. While taking into consideration negative antecedent of U&G theory – irritation, it was decided to start engagement with updating posts on SNS only 1-2 times a week and posting new blog 2-3 times a week.

9.   Empirical research revealed that target audience is engaged with blog reading, moreover behavioral characteristics of youth audience prompt that this group is more easily affected by opinion leaders. Therefore it was decided to make barter agreements with most influencial Latvian blogers. In this way brand Z will be visible on places where target audience is gathering while approximate costs of this kind of promotion campaign are estimated to be 800Eur/year.

References

Augostino, R. (2007). *Social media for business* (p. 10). USA: LuLu.

Banfield, J. (2013, October 28). How Can I Get a Celebrity Level Klout Score of 70 ? Retrieved January 4, 2015, from http://www.warriorforum.com/social-media/861885-how-can-i-get-celebrity-level-klout-score-70-a.html

Brand 4 Baltic – Sector Overview. (2012, January 1). Retrieved December 11, 2014, from http://www.brand4baltic.lt/en/2013/sectors-2/clothing-and-footwear-2/sector-overview-13

Brand 4 Baltic. (2010). Study report on franchising attractiveness of Lithuanian and Latvian border regions. (ISBN: 978-609-95284-4-1).

Bhattacharya, C. (2006). *Services Marketing* (First ed., p. 310). New Delhi: Excel Books.

Brown, E. (2012). *Working the crowd social media marketing for business* (2nd ed., pp. 16-39). London: BCS.

Cass, A. (n.d.). Consumer Self-monitoring, Materialism and Involvement in Fashion Clothing.*Australasian Marketing Journal (AMJ),* 46-60.

Choo-Hui Park & Yong June Kim (2013). Intensity of social network use by involvement: A study of young Chinese users. *International Journal of Business and Management,* 6, 22-33. doi: 10.5539/ijbm.v8n6p22

Consolidated annual report (2013, December 31) *APB Apranga*

Consolidated annual report for 2012 (2013, April) *LPP S.A. Capital Group*

Consultancy, C. (2012, January 16). Draugiem.lv. Retrieved December 9, 2014, from http://cormackconsocial-media-in-latvia/

Consultancy, C. (2011, August 12). Draugiem.lv. Retrieved December 9, 2014, from http://cormackconsultancy.co.uk/tag/social-media-in-latvia/

Cormack Consultancy. (n.d.). Services. Retrieved January 4, 2015, from http://cormackconsultancy.co.uk/services/

Consumer barometer (2013) *People who purchased the product/service online.* Retrieved from http://www.consumerbarometer2013.com/#?app=graph&req=getMetricData& metricId=2&productId=4&countryId=17,18,19

Dahlen, M., Lange, F., & Smith, T. (2010). *Marketing communications: A brand narrative approach* (p. 277). Chichester, U.K.: Wiley.

Ernoult, E. (2013, March 18). 6 Facebook Metrics Marketers Should Be Measuring. Retrieved December 16, 2014, from http://www.socialmediaexaminer.com/facebook-page-metrics/

Euromonitor International (2014, March 10) *Non- grocery retailers in Latvia.* Retrieved from www.portal.euromonitor.com/Portal/Pages/Search/SearchResultsList.aspx

Eurostat. *Youth in Europe: A statistical portrait* (2009 ed.). (2009), pp. 138-160 Luxembourg: Publications Office of the European Union.

Folz, D. H., (1996). Survey Research for Public Administration, p.p. 50, 51. SAGE Publications

George, D., & Mallery, P. (2003). SPSS for Windows step by step: A simple guide and reference. 11.0 update (4th ed.). Boston: Allyn & Bacon

Georgios Tsimonis , Sergios Dimitriadis , (2014) "Brand strategies in social media", Marketing Intelligence & Planning, Vol. 32 Iss: 3, pp.328 – 344

Grinkevičius, P. (2013, July 19) Apranga group CEO Rimantas Perveneckas:"Let's be honest – 80% of what H&M offers well-priced primitive products. Retrieved from http://www.15min.lt/en/article/business/apranga-group-ceo-rimantas-perveneckas-let- s-be-honest-80-percent-of-what-h-m-offers-are-well-priced-primitive-products- 527-354993

Gunter, B., & Furnham, A. (1992). *Consumer profiles: An introduction to psychographics.* London: Routledge

House, J.S. (1981). *Work Stress and Social Support.* Reading, Mass: Addison-Wesley

Indvik, L. (2011, May 17). 5 Best Practices for Fashion Retailers on Facebook. Retrieved January 4, 2015, from http://mashable.com/2011/05/16/fashion-brands-facebook/

Yell. Customer's reviews (2010) *Seppala.* Retrieved from http://en.yell.ru/spb/com/seppala_5210219/

Young, A.L. and Quan – Haase, A. (2009). Information revelation and internet privacy concerns on social network sites: A case study of Facebook. In *Proceedings of the 4th International Conference on Communities and Technologies (C&T),* University Park, PA, p. 265-274

Juzefovics, J. (2011, November 9). Mapping Digital Media: Latvia. Retrieved December 11, 2014, from https://www.academia.edu/1138007/Mapping_Digital_Media_Latvia

Kotler, P., & Keller, K. (2009). *Marketing management* (13th ed., p. 4). Upper Saddle River, N.J.: Pearson Prentice Hall.

Latvijas Statistika. Over the year household consumption expenditure has grown by 6.7%. (2014, July 18). Retrieved December 11, 2014, from http://www.csb.gov.lv/en/notikumi/over-year-household-consumption-expenditure-has-grown-67-39652.html

Latvijas Statistika. DSG10. Average monthly wages and salaries by statistical region of Latvia (in euro)-Statistikas datubāzēs. (n.d.). Retrieved December 11, 2014, from http://data.csb.gov.lv/pxweb/en/Sociala/Sociala__ikgad__dsamaksa/DS0100_e uro.px/table/tableViewLayout1/?rxid=89fa53c2-5ff7-456f-aae4-c4274cf3b2aa

Latvijas Statistika. (n.d.). ISG16. Men and Women by age group at the beginning of year by statistical regions (by 5-year age groups)-Statistikas datubāzēs. Retrieved December 11, 2014, from

http://data.csb.gov.lv/pxweb/en/Sociala/Sociala__ikgad__iedz__iedzskaits/ISO
160.px/table/tableViewLayout1/?rxid=562c2205-ba57-4130-b63a-
6991f49ab6fe

Luo, X. (n.d.). Uses and Gratifications Theory and E-Consumer Behaviors. *Journal
of Interactive Advertising,* 34-41

Lim, K. (2011). *Internet control and anti-control: An examination of public
deliberation through networked media...* S.l.: Proquest, Umi Dissertatio.

Magie, A. (2008). *An analysis of lifestyle, shopping orientations, shopping behaviors
and fashion involvement among teens aged 13 to 18 in the United States* (p. 55)

Malciute, J. (2012, August 1). Customer brand engagement on online social media
platforms: A conceptual model and empirical analysis. Retrieved December 11,
2014, from http://medarbejdere.au.dk/pure/

McCleary, J. (2014, June 6). How to Determine Your Social Media Marketing
Budget. Retrieved December 16, 2014, from
https://www.linkedin.com/pulse/20140607035153-119561274-how-to-
determine-your-social-media-marketing-budget?trk=mp-reader-card

McFatter D. R. (2005). Fashion involvement of affluent female customers. A Thesis.
Louisiana State University

McQuail, D., Blumler, J. G., & Browmn, J. (1972). The television audience: A
revised perspective. In D. McQuail (Ed.), *Sociology of Mass
Communication* (p. 65-130). Middlesex, England: Penguin

Mercedes-Benz Fashion Week. (n.d.). Retrieved December 15, 2014, from
http://mbfashionweek.com/designers/diesel-black-gold

Moss D., Warnaby G., Thame L., (1996) "Tactical publicity or strategic relationship
management? An exploratory investigation of the role of public relations in the
UK retail sector", European Journal of Marketing, Vol. 30 Iss: 12, pp.69 – 84

Official company's website. http://www.apranga.lt/

Okdie M. Bradley (2011). Blogging and self-disclosure: the role of anonymity, self awareness, and perceived audience. The University of Alabama

Rožukalne, A. (n.d.). Media audience development in Latvia (2004-2012). *Media Transformations,* (ISSN 2029-865X doi://10.7220/2029-865X.06.06), 144-157. Retrieved December 11, 2014, from http://www.balticmedia.eu/sites/default/files/MT6_1_144-157.pdf

Saeima (1999, December 20) *Advertising law.* Retrieved from http://www.ptac.gov.lv/upload/normativi_en/reklamas_likums.pdf

Sauer, J. (2013, September 23). Google Analytics 101 for Bloggers, My Blog Elevated Presentation. Retrieved January 4, 2015, from http://www.jeffalytics.com/google-analytics-for-bloggers-presentation/

Safko, L., & Brake, D. (2009). *The social media bible: Tactics, tools, and strategies for business success.* Hoboken, N.J.: John Wiley & Sons.

Scott, D.(2011). *The new rules of marketing & PR: How to use social media, online video, mobile applications, blogs, news releases, & viral marketing to reach buyers directly* (3rd ed.). Hoboken, N.J.: John Wiley & Sons.

Social media guide. (n.d.). Retrieved December 11, 2014, from http://businessculture.org/eastern-europe/latvia/social-media-guide/

Statustor (n.d.). Retrieved November 20, 2014, from http://www.statstutor.ac.uk/resources/uploaded/spearmans.pdf

Stelzner, M. (2013, May 1). 2013 Social media marketing industry report. Retrieved December 11, 2014, from http://www.socialmediaexaminer.com/SocialMediaMarketingIndustryReport20 13.pdf

Sweeney, S., & Craig, R. (2011). *Social media for business 101 ways to grow your business without wasting your time* (p. 13). Gulf Breeze, FL: Maximum Press :.

Transparency International (2009) The most corrupt countries in the world. Retrieved from http://www.ranker.com/list/the-most-corrupt-countries-in-the-world/info-lists

Tsimonis G., Dimitriadis S, (2014), *Brand strategies in social media*, Marketing Intelligence & Planning, Vol. 32 Iss 3 pp. 328 – 344 Retrieved from: http://dx.doi.org/10.1108/MIP-04-2013-0056

Tuten, T., & Solomon, M. (2013). *Social media marketing* (pp. 102-120).

Waddington, S. (2012). *Share this: The social media handbook for PR professionals.* Chichester: John Wiley & Sons.

Zaichkowsky (1985). Measuring the involvement construct. *Journal of Consumer Research,* 12, 341-352.

Appendixes

Appendix 1. Retail turnover of company's stores by chains (EUR)

Chain	2013 (EUR)	Procentage
Economy	16.7 million	9.87%
Youth	57.2 million	33.7%
Business	24.6 million	14.5%
Luxury	20.22 million	11.9%
Zara	44.28 million	26.1%
Outlets	6.2 million	3.67%
Total	169.25 million	~100%

Resource: Consolidated annual report of the company (2013, December 31)

Appendix 2. Internet activities (as a % of individuals by age group)

	16-24	25-34	35-44	45-54
Communication	94	91	87	85
Sending / receiving emails	89	88	84	82
Advanced communication services	83	65	49	43
Information search and online services	95	96	93	91
Finding information about goods and services	74	86	84	82
Training and education	72	57	51	47
Downloading software	42	36	27	23
Using services related to travel and accommodation	41	57	55	55
Reading / downloading online newspapers / news magazines	40	46	41	39
Banking, the selling of goods or services	37	60	56	51
Seeking health information on injury, disease or nutrition	33	49	48	48
Looking for a job or sending a job application	28	30	20	15
Leisure activities related to obtaining and sharing audiovisual content	84	69	55	47
Downloading / listening to / watching / playing music, films and/or games	78	58	43	35
Peer-to-peer file sharing for exchanging movies, music, video files	24	15	7	5
Using podcast service to automatically receive audio or video files of interest	10	8	5	3
Interaction with public authorities	33	51	50	49
Obtaining information from public authorities web sites	28	46	46	45
Downloading official forms	17	30	29	28
Sending filled forms	12	22	21	21

Resource: Eurostat. *Youth in Europe: A statistical portrait* (2009 ed.). (2009), pp. 138-160 Luxembourg: Publications Office of the European Union.

Appendix 3. Full questionnaire that was provided for respondents

Norādiet informāciju par sevi:

Dzimums [....] ▾
Vecums   [---] ▾

Turpināt

1. Jūsu dzīvesvieta:

☐ Rīga
☐ Pierīga
☐ Daugavpils
☐ Jelgava
☐ Jēkabpils
☐ Jūrmala
☐ Liepāja
☐ Rēzekne
☐ Valmiera
☐ Ventspils
☐ Cita pilsēta vai mazpilsēta
☐ Lauki

Turpināt

IMPROVEMENT OF SOCIAL MEDIA COMMUNICATION

4%

2. Apmēram, cik daudz laika dienā Jūs pavadāt sociālajos tīklos?

☐ Mazāk kā 30 minūtes
☐ 30 minūtes līdz vienai stundai
☐ 2-3 stundas
☐ Vairāk kā 3 stundas
☐ Nelietoju sociālos tīklus

[Turpināt]

9%

3. Kurus sociālos tīklus Jūs lietojat? Lūdzu atzīmējiet tos, kuros Jūs esat reģistrējies ilgāk par 3 mēnešiem. (vairākas atbildes iespējamas)

☐ Facebook
☐ Instagram
☐ Pinterest
☐ Twitter
☐ MySpace
☐ Google+
☐ LinkedIn
☐ Draugiem.lv
☐ Nevienu

[Turpināt]

IMPROVEMENT OF SOCIAL MEDIA COMMUNICATION

4. Lūdzu, atzīmējiet, kurš no šiem apgalvojumiem par blogiem attiecas uz Jums:

☐ Es rakstu savu blogu un lasu arī citus blogus

☐ Es rakstu savu blogu, bet nelasu citus blogus

☐ Es lasu blogus, taču nerakstu pats savējo

☐ Es zinu kas ir blogi, taču es tos nelasu un arī pats nerakstu

☐ Es nezinu kas ir blogs

Turpināt

5. Cik lielā mērā Jums patīk sociālajos tīklos pasniegtā informācija sekojošos veidos:

	1 – Nepatīk	2	3	4	5 – Ļoti patīk
Bildes, fotogrāfijas	☐	☐	☐	☐	☐
Video	☐	☐	☐	☐	☐
Audio faili	☐	☐	☐	☐	☐
Raksts blogā	☐	☐	☐	☐	☐
Īsa, kodolīga ziņa	☐	☐	☐	☐	☐

Turpināt

22%

6. Lūdzu, novērtējiet, cik lielā mērā Jūs piekrītat šiem apgalvojumiem:

	1 - Nepiekrītu	2	3	4	5 - Piekrītu
Izmantot sociālos tīklus ir izklaidējoši	☐	☐	☐	☐	☐
Soc. tīkli ir labs veids, kā kontaktēties ar draugiem	☐	☐	☐	☐	☐
Ir interesanti skatīties citu cilvēku statusu un informāciju, kas izvietota viņu soc. tīklu lapās	☐	☐	☐	☐	☐
Soc. tīkli ir noderīgi	☐	☐	☐	☐	☐
Esmu atvērts dalīties ar savu personīgu informāciju soc. tīklos	☐	☐	☐	☐	☐
Soc. tīklu izmantošana ir droša un uzticama	☐	☐	☐	☐	☐
Soc. tīklu izmantošana var kaitēt attiecībām	☐	☐	☐	☐	☐
Dodu priekšroku komunikācijai klātienē, nekā komunikācijai caur soc. tīkliem	☐	☐	☐	☐	☐
Man patīk publicēt un dalīties ar fotogrāfijām/bildēm soc. tīklos	☐	☐	☐	☐	☐

Turpināt

26%

7. Lūdzu, novērtējiet, cik lielā mērā Jūs piekrītat šiem apgalvojumiem:

	1 - Nepiekrītu	2	3	4	5 - Piekrītu
Mani interesē un es apmeklēju dažādas soc. tīklu uzņēmumu un zīmolu veidotās lapas	☐	☐	☐	☐	☐
Man ir pietiekami daudz laika, lai skatītos uzņēmumu publicēto informāciju sociālajos tīklos	☐	☐	☐	☐	☐
Man patīk iegūt/uzzināt uzņēmumu publicēto informāciju sociālajos tīklos	☐	☐	☐	☐	☐
Es apmeklēju uzņēmumu sociālo tīklu lapas, jo man interesē vairāk uzzināt par šo uzņēmumu/zīmolu	☐	☐	☐	☐	☐

Turpināt

30%

8. Kas Jūs motivē sekot/pierakstīties uzņēmumu sociālo tīklu lapām?

	1 - NEmotivē	2	3	4	5 - Motivē
Iespēja lasīt uzņēmuma jaunumus / informāciju	☐	☐	☐	☐	☐
Iespēja piedalīties uzņēmuma veidotajās izlozēs	☐	☐	☐	☐	☐
Sajūta, ka esmu piederīgs šim zīmolam un citiem šī zīmola sekotājiem	☐	☐	☐	☐	☐
Iespēja saņemt klientu atbalstu, kad tas nepieciešams	☐	☐	☐	☐	☐
Iespēja iesniegt savas idejas un piedalīties jaunu produktu attīstībā	☐	☐	☐	☐	☐
Iespēja iegūt atlaides	☐	☐	☐	☐	☐
Būt vienam no pirmajiem, kas uzzina uzņēmuma jaunumus / informāciju	☐	☐	☐	☐	☐
Uzzināt vairāk informāciju par uzņēmuma produktiem / pakalpojumiem	☐	☐	☐	☐	☐

Turpināt

35%

9. Kāds Jums ir pieņemamākais veids kā iegūt informāciju par uzņēmumu / zīmolu sociālajos tīklos?

☐ Lasīt ziņas un vēsturi par uzņēmumu un produktiem

☐ Lasīt citu cilvēku teikto par šo uzņēmumu un produktiem

☐ Skatīties bildes un video par šo uzņēmumu un produktiem

Turpināt

90

39%

10. Kāda veida reklāmas Jums ir vairāk pieņemamas, kas izvietotas sociālajos tīklos?

	1 - NEpiekrītu	2	3	4	5 - Piekrītu
Man patīk, ka man vispirms pajautā, vai vēlēšos saņemt uzņēmuma izvietoto informāciju un reklāmas soc. tīklos	☐	☐	☐	☐	☐
Man patīk saņemt personalizētu, man aktuālu informāciju un reklāmas, ja tas nav biežāk kā reizi nedēļā	☐	☐	☐	☐	☐
Es nekad nepiekrītu saņemt informāciju vai reklāmas no uzņēmumiem, ja man ir iespēja izvēlēties	☐	☐	☐	☐	☐
Reklāmas, kas tiek rādītas TV - dažādu filmu un pārraižu vidū, ir kaitinošas un es parasti tās ignorēju	☐	☐	☐	☐	☐
No TV un žurnālu reklāmām, es parasti uzzinu ko jaunu par reklamēto produktu	☐	☐	☐	☐	☐

Turpināt

43%

11. Kāda veida informācija no uzņēmumiem sociālajos tīklos Jums ir noderīga visvairāk?

	1 - Nav noderīga	2	3	4	5	6	7	8	9	10 - Ļoti noderīga
Paziņojumi par atlaidēm un izpārdošanām	☐	☐	☐	☐	☐	☐	☐	☐	☐	☐
Ziņas no konkrētās jomas ekspertiem / profesionāļiem	☐	☐	☐	☐	☐	☐	☐	☐	☐	☐
Informācija par jauniem produktiem / veikaliem	☐	☐	☐	☐	☐	☐	☐	☐	☐	☐
Ekskluzīvu informāciju par zīmoliem / produktiem	☐	☐	☐	☐	☐	☐	☐	☐	☐	☐
Citu cilvēku izvietoto informāciju vai viedokli par šo zīmolu / produktiem	☐	☐	☐	☐	☐	☐	☐	☐	☐	☐

Turpināt

IMPROVEMENT OF SOCIAL MEDIA COMMUNICATION

48%

12. Jūsuprāt, kas visvairāk veicina cilvēku piederību konkrētam zīmolam un citiem šī zīmola sekotājiem sociālajos tīklos?

	1 - Pilnīgi NEpiekrītu	2	3	4	5 - Pilnīgi piekrītu
Dalība lēmumu pieņemšanā	☐	☐	☐	☐	☐
Diskusijas	☐	☐	☐	☐	☐
Ikdienišķas sarunas	☐	☐	☐	☐	☐
Iespēja dalīties ar savu pieredzi par šo zīmolu	☐	☐	☐	☐	☐

Turpināt

52%

13. Kādās izlozēs Jūs gribētu piedalīties?
Iespēja vinnēt balvas, ja...

☐ ... dalos ar sevis izvēlēto apģērbu salikumu no konkrētā apģērbu veikala

☐ ... izveidoju promo video par kādu reklāmu / uzņēmumu

☐ ... izdomāju uzņēmuma vai produkta saukli / nosaukumu

☐ ... izveidot krāsu kombiāciju jaunās sezonas apģērbiem no konkrētā apģērbu veikala

☐ Es negribētu piedalīties uzņēmumu veidotajās izlozēs

Turpināt

57%

14. Ko Jūs darītu, ja zināms zīmols izsludinātu konkursu un iespēju vinnēt balvas? Daliba konkursā ir tiem, kas izveido savu video par šo zīmolu un pubilcē to sociālajā tīklā?

☐ Es izveidotu savu video un publicētu to savā soc. tīkla lapā

☐ Es balsotu un vērtētu citu video, taču par savu video neveidotu

☐ Es izteiktu viedokli un komentētu citu izveidotos video

☐ Es dalītos ar citu veidotajiem video

☐ Es apskatītu šos video, taču neveiktu nekādas citas darbības

☐ Šāds konkurss manu uzmanību vispār nepievērstu

[Turpināt]

61%

15. Jūsuprāt, kāds ir optimāls biežums jaunu ierakstu publicēšanai sociālajos tīklos?

☐ 2 rezies dienā

☐ Reizi dienā

☐ Katru otro dienu

☐ 1-2 reizes nedēļā

☐ Retāk

[Turpināt]

93

IMPROVEMENT OF SOCIAL MEDIA COMMUNICATION

16. Cik lielā mērā Jūs saistītu šādi apģērbu zīmola ieraksti soc. tīklu lapās:

	1 - Nesaistītu nemaz	2	3	4	5 - Ļoti saistītu
Diskusijas par jaunumiem modes pasaulē	☐	☑	☐	☐	☐
Veiksmīgākās apģērbu kombinācijas	☐	☑	☐	☐	☐
Labas rīta/dienas vēlējums	☐	☑	☐	☐	☐
Spārnoti izteicieni	☐	☑	☐	☐	☐
Izklaidējošs, smieklīgs ieraksts	☐	☑	☐	☐	☐

Turpināt

17. Kā Jūs vērtētu savu interesi par modi?

	1 - NEpiekrītu	2	3	4	5 - Piekrītu
Mani ļoti interesē mode un apģērbs	☐	☐	☐	☐	☐
Es piedomāju pie tā kādu apģērbu izvēlos un valkāju. Man ir svarīgi kā izskatos	☐	☐	☐	☐	☐
Man ir svarīgi iegādāties modīgu apģērbu	☐	☐	☐	☐	☐
Mans apģērbs un stils ir viens no veidiem, kā demonstrēt sevi / savu būtību	☐	☐	☐	☐	☐
Man ir svarīgs tēls, ko par cilvēku rada modīgs apģērbs	☐	☐	☐	☐	☐
Man sagādā prieku, valkājot modīgu apģērbu	☐	☐	☐	☐	☐
Izvēloties apģērbu, man ir svarīgi, ka varēšu šo apģērbu valkāt ilgu laiku	☐	☐	☐	☐	☐

Turpināt

IMPROVEMENT OF SOCIAL MEDIA COMMUNICATION

/4%

18. Cik lielā mērā Jūs sekojat līdzi modes tendencēm?

☐ Es sekoju līdzi modes tendencēm un arī atbilstoši atjaunoju / papildinu savu garderobi
☐ Es sekoju līdzi modes tendencēm, taču ne vienmēr izvēlos atģērbu atbilstoši šīm tendencēm
☐ Es apskatos ka šobrīd ir modē tikai tad, kad iegādājos jaunu apģērbu
☐ Kopumā es nesekoju līdzi modes tendencēm, izņemot gadījumus, kad tendences mainās būtiski
☐ Mani vispār neinteresē modes tendences

Turpināt

78%

19. Cik modes ekspertu lapām sociālajos medijos Jūs sekojat?

☐ 0
☐ 1-5
☐ 5-10
☐ Vairāk kā 10

Turpināt

IMPROVEMENT OF SOCIAL MEDIA COMMUNICATION

83%

20. Kuru apģērbu zīmolu lapām sociālajos medijos Jūs sekojat? (vairākas atbildes iespējamas)

☐ Zara
☐ H&M
☐ House
☐ Denim Dream
☐ Mohito
☐ Reserved
☐ Pull&Bear
☐ Bershka
☐ Seppala
☐ Mango
☐ Guess
☐ Nesekoju nevienam

Turpināt

87%

21. Vai Jūs šobrid sekojat Moskito zīmolu lapai sociālajos tīklos?

☐ Jā
☐ Esmu redzējis šī zīmola aktivitātes soc. tīklos, taču nesekoju
☐ Neesmu redzējis šī zīmola aktivitātes soc. tīklos, taču man būtu interese sekot
☐ Neesmu redzējis šī zīmola aktivitātes soc. tīklos un man nebūtu interese sekot

Turpināt

96

IMPROVEMENT OF SOCIAL MEDIA COMMUNICATION

96%

23. Jūsu ienākumu līmenis (mēnesi, pēc nodokļu nomaksas):

☐ Līdz 350 EUR
☐ 351-500 EUR
☐ 501-800 EUR
☐ 801-1200 EUR
☐ Vairāk kā 1200 EUR
☐ Nav ienākumu
☐ Nevēlos norādīt

Turpināt

Survey

Gender (highlight):

Male

Female

Age (highlight):

< 25;

25-34

over 35

IMPROVEMENT OF SOCIAL MEDIA COMMUNICATION

1. Place of living:

☐ Riga   ☐ Rezekne

☐ Pieriga   ☐ Valmiera

☐ Daugavpils   ☐ Ventspils

☐ Jelgava   ☐ Lauki

☐ Jekabpils

☐ Jurmala

☐ Liepaja

1. How much time do you spend on social media per day on average?

☐ < 30 mins

☐ 30mins – 1hour

☐ 2-3 hours

☐ More than 3 hours

☐ I do not use social media at all

2. Which social media networking platforms are you using not less than 3months, if any? You may select more than one answer.

☐ Facebook   ☐ LinkedIn

☐ Instagram   ☐ Draugiem.lv

☐ Pinterest   ☐ None

☐ Twitter

☐ MySpace

☐ Google+

3. Which statement best describes you?

☐ I write my own blogs and read other people's blogs;

☐ I write my own blogs but do not read other people's blogs;

□ I read other people's blogs, but do not write my own;

□ I know what blog is, but do not read or write them

□I do not know what blog is.

4. How these ways of presenting information within social media are attractive for you?

	Not attractive 1	2	3	4	Very attractive 5
Uploaded picture	□	□	□	□	□
Video	□	□	□	□	□
Digital media file (audio)	□	□	□	□	□
Detailed story provided in a Blog form	□	□	□	□	□
Short message/ tweet	□	□	□	□	□

5. Evaluate how much do you agree with these statements?

	Strongly Disagree 1	2	3	4	Strongly Agree 5
Using social media is entertaining	□	□	□	□	□
Social media it is a good way to keep in touch with friends	□	□	□	□	□
It is interesting to check others status and information	□	□	□	□	□

through social media					
Social networking is useful	☐	☐	☐	☐	☐
I am willing to share personal information on social media	☐	☐	☐	☐	☐
Using social media is safe and secure	☐	☐	☐	☐	☐
Social networking can harm relationships	☐	☐	☐	☐	☐
I prefer face-to-face communication rather than using the Internet	☐	☐	☐	☐	☐
I like sharing photos through social networking systems	☐	☐	☐	☐	☐

6. How much do you agree with the following statements?

	Strongly Disagree 1	2	3	4	Strongly Agree 5
I browse on fan pages within social media because I am interested in being part of brand community	☐	☐	☐	☐	☐
I have enough time to browse on social media fan	☐	☐	☐	☐	☐

pages					
I enjoy browsing on social media fan pages	☐	☐	☐	☐	☐
I browse on social media fan pages because I am interested in the brands they are dedicated to	☐	☐	☐	☐	☐

7. Evaluate how strongly it motivates you to follow brand's/ company's page on social media platforms?

	Do not motivates at all 1	2	3	4	Motivates very much 5
Possibility to read reviews	☐	☐	☐	☐	☐
Chance to take part in contests	☐	☐	☐	☐	☐
Belonging to certain community	☐	☐	☐	☐	☐
Getting customer service when needed	☐	☐	☐	☐	☐
Chance to submit ideas for new product or brand's development	☐	☐	☐	☐	☐
Discounts	☐	☐	☐	☐	☐
Getting exclusive information first	☐	☐	☐	☐	☐
Learning about	☐	☐	☐	☐	☐

new products					

8. What is the most acceptable way for you to learn about product/brand in social media?

☐ By hearing stories, product history

☐ By collecting opinion of others about product/brand

☐ By seeing pictures, videos of product/ brand

9. Which kind of advertising is more acceptable for you?

	Strongly disagree 1	2	3	4	Strongly agree 5
I like when I am asked if I want to receive information on products and to see certain adds on social media	☐	☐	☐	☐	☐
I like to get personalized information on products through email and social media, as long as it is not more than once a week	☐	☐	☐	☐	☐
I never agree to get more information on products when I am asked on social media	☐	☐	☐	☐	☐

Advertisement that shows up in the middle of the movie on TV are annoying and I usually ignore them	☐	☐	☐	☐	☐
By seeing advertisements on TV and magazines I learn about new products	☐	☐	☐	☐	☐

10. Which information on social media pages is most beneficial for you?

	Not beneficial at all 1	2	3	4	5	6	7	8	9	Very much beneficial 10
Information on sales and discounts	☐	☐	☐	☐	☐	☐	☐	☐	☐	☐
Experts/ professionals insights and ideas	☐	☐	☐	☐	☐	☐	☐	☐	☐	☐
New product releases/ store openings	☐	☐	☐	☐	☐	☐	☐	☐	☐	☐
Behind the scenes information	☐	☐	☐	☐	☐	☐	☐	☐	☐	☐
Problems and questions that other face with	☐	☐	☐	☐	☐	☐	☐	☐	☐	☐

the same product/service you like									

11. What in your opinion strengthens "community" feeling within social spaces the most?

	Strongly disagree 1	2	3	4	Strongly agree 5
Involvement to decision making	☐	☐	☐	☐	☐
Discussions	☐	☐	☐	☐	☐
Every day conversations	☐	☐	☐	☐	☐
Ability to share your problems, photos, questions within social media page	☐	☐	☐	☐	☐

12. In which contest you will most likely take place?
   ☐ Sharing your style combinations with clothes from certain store
   ☐ Creating a promotional video for some product/brand
   ☐ Creating a slogan for certain brand
   ☐ Paint your imaginative next seasons clothes collection
   ☐ I would not participate on any contest within social media

13. What would be your actions if your favorite brand will publish a contest within social media page, where you have to create video and post it in order to participate?

□ You will participate in contest by creating a video and will share your link in order to win competition

□ You will rate and vote on videos created, but do not participate yourself

□ You will express your opinion by commenting on posted videos

□You will share the video that you like/dislike the most, so others can see/laugh

□ You will take a look what is going on, but do not participate, comment or vote

□ It will not grab your attention at all

14. What in your opinion is optimal frequency for new post/tweet?

□ 2 times a day

□ Once a day

□ Every second day

□ 1-2 times a week

□ Rarely

15. If clothing brand page on social media would post once a day, how you would evaluate engagement with post?

	Not likely to engage 1	2	3	4	Very likely to engage 5
Discussion about day's news within fashion business	□	□	□	□	□
Clothes combination for a day	□	□	□	□	□
Good morning	□	□	□	□	□

message					
Motivational quotation	☐	☐	☐	☐	☐
Message with funny content	☐	☐	☐	☐	☐

16. How would you evaluate your involvement to fashion?

	Strongly disagree 1	2	3	4	Strongly agree 5
I am very interested in fashion clothing	☐	☐	☐	☐	☐
I think a lot about my choices when it comes to fashion clothing	☐	☐	☐	☐	☐
Purchasing fashion clothing is significant to me	☐	☐	☐	☐	☐
Fashion clothing helps me to express who I really am	☐	☐	☐	☐	☐
My main concern is the image that fashion clothes has	☐	☐	☐	☐	☐
Wearing fashion clothing gives me a lot of pleasure	☐	☐	☐	☐	☐
All what matters to me when wearing fashion clothing is durability	☐	☐	☐	☐	☐

17. Which one of the statements describes the best your reaction to changing fashions in clothes?

□ I read fashion news regularly and try to keep my wardrobe up to date with the fashion trends

□I keep to date on all the fashion trends although I do not always attempt to dress according those trends

□I check to see what is currently fashionable only when I need to buy some new clothes

□I do not pay much attention to fashion trends unless major change takes place

□ I am not interested to fashion trends at all

18. How many fashion opinion leaders are you following/ subscribing within social media platforms?

□ 0

□ 1-5

□ 5-10

□ more than 10

19. Which other clothing brands are you following on social media platforms?

□ Zara   □ Bershka

□ H&M   □ Seppala

□ House   □ Mango

□ Denim Dream   □ Guess

□ Mohito   □ I am not following any

□ Reserved

□ Pull&Bear

IMPROVEMENT OF SOCIAL MEDIA COMMUNICATION

20. Are you currently engaged with brand Z on social media platforms?

☐ Yes

☐ I have seen this brand on social media platforms but I haven't joined

☐ Never saw this brand on social media platforms, but I would like to join

☐ Never saw this brand on social media platforms and I also do not want to join

21. For the ones who answered YES (Question 21) Could you please evaluate engagement with brand Z on Facebook page:

	Strongly disagree 1	2	3	4	Strongly agree 5
I like that new collections are presented by wearing clothes on the stores	☐	☐	☐	☐	☐
I would like to see prices together with every picture	☐	☐	☐	☐	☐
Stories told within social media page are not encouraging	☐	☐	☐	☐	☐
Page would be more interactive if people could share how clothes bought in this store looks on them	☐	☐	☐	☐	☐
social media page of brand Z has strong social	☐	☐	☐	☐	☐

108

community						

22.Personal monthly income, after taxes:

□ Till 350Eur

□ 351-500Eur

□ 501-800Eur

□801-1200Eur

□ More than 1200Eur

□ No income

□ Do not know/ refuse to answer

Appendix 4. Descriptive statistics

Question 5. Blogging preferences

Phlogging		Vlogging		Podcasts		Social blogs		Microblogging	
Mean	4,05	Mean	3,55	Mean	2,89	Mean	3,04	Mean	3,98
Standard Error	0,06	Standard Error	0,07	Standard Error	0,08	Standard Error	0,07	Standard Error	0,07
Median	4,00	Median	4,00	Median	3,00	Median	3,00	Median	4,00
Mode	4,00	Mode	4,00	Mode	3,00	Mode	3,00	Mode	4,00
Standard Deviation	0,89	Standard Deviation	0,93	Standard Deviation	1,08	Standard Deviation	1,06	Standard Deviation	0,96
Sample Variance	0,79	Sample Variance	0,87	Sample Variance	1,17	Sample Variance	1,12	Sample Variance	0,92
Kurtosis	0,45	Kurtosis	0,22	Kurtosis	-0,55	Kurtosis	-0,71	Kurtosis	-0,13
Skewness	-0,81	Skewness	-0,46	Skewness	0,06	Skewness	-0,05	Skewness	-0,70
Range	4,00	Range	4,00	Range	4,00	Range	4,00	Range	4,00
Minimum	1,00	Minimum	1,00	Minimum	1,00	Minimum	1,00	Minimum	1,00
Maximum	5,00	Maximum	5,00	Maximum	5,00	Maximum	5,00	Maximum	5,00
Sum	830,00	Sum	728,00	Sum	592,00	Sum	623,00	Sum	816,00
Count	205,00	Count	205,00	Count	205,00	Count	205,00	Count	205,00

Social media involvement Question 6

Personal		Personal		personal		Personal		Physical		Physical		Situational		Situational		Personal	
Mean	3,94	Mean	4	Mean	3,45	Mean	3,90	Mean	2,54	Mean	2,29	Mean	3,30	Mean	3,88	Mean	2,83
Standard Error	0,06	Standard Error	0,06810968	Standard Error	0,08	Standard Error	0,06	Standard Error	0,08	Standard Erro	0,07	Standard Erro	0,07	Standard Erro	0,07	Standard Erro	0,09
Median	4,00	Median	4	Median	3,00	Median	4,00	Median	2,00	Median	2,00	Median	3,00	Median	4,00	Median	3,00
Mode	5,00	Mode	5	Mode	3,00	Mode	4,00	Mode	3,00	Mode	2,00	Mode	4,00	Mode	5,00	Mode	3,00
Standard Deviation	0,92	Standard Deviation	0,97518224	Standard Deviation	1,09	Standard Deviation	0,87	Standard Deviation	1,14	Standard Dev	1,05	Standard Dev	1,06	Standard Dev	1,03	Standard Dev	1,24
Sample Variance	0,85	Sample Variance	0,95098039	Sample Variance	1,18	Sample Variance	0,76	Sample Variance	1,30	Sample Varia	1,10	Sample Varia	1,12	Sample Varia	1,06	Sample Varia	1,54
Kurtosis	-0,37	Kurtosis	-0,0191101	Kurtosis	-0,47	Kurtosis	-0,44	Kurtosis	-0,53	Kurtosis	-0,15	Kurtosis	-0,51	Kurtosis	-0,41	Kurtosis	-0,35
Skewness	-0,45	Skewness	-0,73663	Skewness	-0,32	Skewness	-0,34	Skewness	0,38	Skewness	0,60	Skewness	-0,28	Skewness	-0,54	Skewness	0,07
Range	4,00	Range	4	Range	4,00	Range	4,00	Range	4,00	Range	4,00	Range	4,00	Range	4,00	Range	4,00
Minimum	1,00	Minimum	1	Minimum	1,00	Minimum	1,00	Minimum	1,00	Minimum	1,00	Minimum	1,00	Minimum	1,00	Minimum	1,00
Maximum	5,00	Maximum	5	Maximum	5,00	Maximum	5,00	Maximum	5,00	Maximum	5,00	Maximum	5,00	Maximum	5,00	Maximum	5,00
Sum	808,00	Sum	820	Sum	709,00	Sum	799,00	Sum	520,00	Sum	470,00	Sum	677,00	Sum	799,00	Sum	580,00
Count	205,00	Count	205	Count	205,00	Count	205,00	Count	205,00	Count	205,00	Count	205,00	Count	205,00	Count	205,00

Motives for usage Question 8

109

	Reviews		Contests		Community		Customer service		Submit ideas		Discounts		Exclusive information		Learning about products	
Mean	3,4926829	Mean	3,6243902	Mean	2,6829268	Mean	3,195122	Mean	2,7317073	Mean	3,7609756	Mean	3,3170732	Mean	3,6341463
Standard Er	0,0834512	Standard Er	0,0872117	Standard Er	0,0821737	Standard Error	0,0838737	Standard Error	0,0806639	Standard Error	0,0834582	Standard Error	0,0807056	Standard Error	0,0760014
Median	4	Median	4	Median	3	Median	3	Median	3	Median	4	Median	3	Median	4
Mode	4	Mode	5	Mode	3	Mode	3	Mode	3	Mode	5	Mode	3	Mode	4
Standard D	1,1948399	Standard D	1,2486818	Standard D	1,1765483	Standard Deviatio	1,2008884	Standard Deviatio	1,1552181	Standard Deviation	1,1949399	Standard Deviation	1,1555286	Standard Deviatio	1,0881739
Sample Var	1,4276429	Sample Var	1,5592061	Sample Var	1,3842659	Sample Variance	1,442133	Sample Variance	1,3345289	Sample Variance	1,4278814	Sample Variance	1,3352463	Sample Variance	1,1841224
Kurtosis	-0,7056388	Kurtosis	-0,711498	Kurtosis	-0,7091515	Kurtosis	-0,6235541	Kurtosis	-0,5838884	Kurtosis	-0,1191667	Kurtosis	-0,5558855	Kurtosis	-0,0639758
Skewness	-0,4352485	Skewness	-0,5383045	Skewness	0,2010609	Skewness	-0,2450622	Skewness	0,1929215	Skewness	-0,8162046	Skewness	-0,3549677	Skewness	-0,6601466
Range	4	Range	4	Range	4	Range	4	Range	4	Range	4	Range	4	Range	4
Minimum	1	Minimum	1	Minimum	1	Minimum	1	Minimum	1	Minimum	1	Minimum	1	Minimum	1
Maximum	5	Maximum	5	Maximum	5	Maximum	5	Maximum	5	Maximum	5	Maximum	5	Maximum	5
Sum	716	Sum	743	Sum	550	Sum	655	Sum	560	Sum	771	Sum	680	Sum	745
Count	205	Count	205	Count	205	Count	205	Count	205	Count	205	Count	205	Count	205

Customer brand engagement on social media platforms. Question 7.

Goals		Resources		Perceived cost/benefit		Goals	
Mean	3,40	Mean	2,65	Mean	3,20	Mean	3,23
Standard Err	0,08	Standard Err	0,08	Standard Err	0,07	Standard Error	0,08
Median	3,00	Median	3,00	Median	3,00	Median	3,00
Mode	4,00	Mode	3,00	Mode	3,00	Mode	4,00
Standard De	1,16	Standard De	1,10	Standard De	1,06	Standard Deviation	1,21
Sample Varia	1,35	Sample Varia	1,22	Sample Varia	1,13	Sample Variance	1,45
Kurtosis	-0,67	Kurtosis	-0,37	Kurtosis	-0,56	Kurtosis	-0,90
Skewness	-0,32	Skewness	0,34	Skewness	-0,14	Skewness	-0,18
Range	4,00	Range	4,00	Range	4,00	Range	4,00
Minimum	1,00	Minimum	1,00	Minimum	1,00	Minimum	1,00
Maximum	5,00	Maximum	5,00	Maximum	5,00	Maximum	5,00
Sum	696,00	Sum	544,00	Sum	656,00	Sum	662,00
Count	205,00	Count	205,00	Count	205,00	Count	205,00

Marketing techniques. Question 10.

Permission		Permission		Interruption		Permission		Interruption	
Mean	4,44	Mean	3,56	Mean	2,93	Mean	4,05	Mean	2,90
Standard Err	0,06	Standard Err	0,08	Standard Err	0,09	Standard Err	0,08	Standard Err	0,08
Median	5,00	Median	4,00	Median	3,00	Median	5,00	Median	3,00
Mode	5,00	Mode	4,00	Mode	3,00	Mode	5,00	Mode	3,00
Standard De	0,88	Standard De	1,14	Standard De	1,23	Standard De	1,11	Standard De	1,12
Sample Varia	0,77	Sample Varia	1,31	Sample Varia	1,51	Sample Varia	1,24	Sample Varia	1,26
Kurtosis	2,97	Kurtosis	-0,46	Kurtosis	-0,84	Kurtosis	-0,20	Kurtosis	-0,69
Skewness	-1,75	Skewness	-0,51	Skewness	-0,08	Skewness	-0,86	Skewness	-0,12
Range	4,00	Range	4,00	Range	4,00	Range	4,00	Range	4,00
Minimum	1,00	Minimum	1,00	Minimum	1,00	Minimum	1,00	Minimum	1,00
Maximum	5,00	Maximum	5,00	Maximum	5,00	Maximum	5,00	Maximum	5,00
Sum	911,00	Sum	730,00	Sum	601,00	Sum	831,00	Sum	595,00
Count	205,00	Count	205,00	Count	205,00	Count	205,00	Count	205,00

Content relevance. Question 11. Descriptive statistics

Sales/discounts		Esperts insights		New products		Behind the scenes		Problems and questions	
Mean	7,59	Mean	6,49	Mean	6,85	Mean	5,82	Mean	6,43
Standard Err	0,18	Standard Err	0,16	Standard Err	0,16	Standard Err	0,18	Standard Err	0,18
Median	8,00	Median	7,00	Median	7,00	Median	6,00	Median	7,00
Mode	10,00	Mode	8,00	Mode	8,00	Mode	7,00	Mode	7,00
Standard De	2,51	Standard De	2,33	Standard De	2,28	Standard De	2,58	Standard De	2,51
Sample Varia	6,30	Sample Varia	5,41	Sample Varia	5,18	Sample Varia	6,66	Sample Varia	6,31
Kurtosis	-0,06	Kurtosis	-0,35	Kurtosis	-0,53	Kurtosis	-0,84	Kurtosis	-0,72
Skewness	-0,91	Skewness	-0,51	Skewness	-0,49	Skewness	-0,17	Skewness	-0,35
Range	9,00	Range	9,00	Range	9,00	Range	9,00	Range	9,00
Minimum	1,00	Minimum	1,00	Minimum	1,00	Minimum	1,00	Minimum	1,00
Maximum	10,00	Maximum	10,00	Maximum	10,00	Maximum	10,00	Maximum	10,00
Sum	1556,00	Sum	1330,00	Sum	1405,00	Sum	1193,00	Sum	1319,00
Count	205,00	Count	205,00	Count	205,00	Count	205,00	Count	205,00

Motives for community feeling. Question 12

Decision making		Discussions		Everyday conversations		Share ideas/problems	
Mean	3,07	Mean	3,36	Mean	3,30	Mean	3,75
Standard Err	0,08	Standard Err	0,07	Standard Err	0,07	Standard Err	0,07
Median	3,00	Median	3,00	Median	3,00	Median	4,00
Mode	3,00	Mode	3,00	Mode	3,00	Mode	4,00
Standard De	1,12	Standard De	0,98	Standard De	0,98	Standard De	1,05
Sample Varia	1,25	Sample Varia	0,97	Sample Varia	0,96	Sample Varia	1,10
Kurtosis	-0,47	Kurtosis	0,06	Kurtosis	0,03	Kurtosis	-0,13
Skewness	-0,17	Skewness	-0,26	Skewness	-0,19	Skewness	-0,59
Range	4,00	Range	4,00	Range	4,00	Range	4,00
Minimum	1,00	Minimum	1,00	Minimum	1,00	Minimum	1,00
Maximum	5,00	Maximum	5,00	Maximum	5,00	Maximum	5,00
Sum	630,00	Sum	688,00	Sum	677,00	Sum	769,00
Count	205,00	Count	205,00	Count	205,00	Count	205,00

Content relevance (everyday message). Question 16

Fashion news		Clothes combination		Good morning message		Motivational quote		Funny message	
Mean	2,67	Mean	3,23	Mean	3,02	Mean	3,22	Mean	3,53
Standard Err	0,09	Standard Err	0,09	Standard Err	0,09	Standard Err	0,09	Standard Err	0,08
Median	3,00	Median	3,00	Median	3,00	Median	3,00	Median	4,00
Mode	3,00	Mode	4,00	Mode	3,00	Mode	3,00	Mode	4,00
Standard De	1,24	Standard De	1,29	Standard De	1,28	Standard De	1,24	Standard De	1,19
Sample Varia	1,55	Sample Varia	1,67	Sample Varia	1,63	Sample Varia	1,53	Sample Varia	1,41
Kurtosis	-1,00	Kurtosis	-1,00	Kurtosis	-0,92	Kurtosis	-0,87	Kurtosis	-0,48
Skewness	0,19	Skewness	-0,31	Skewness	-0,14	Skewness	-0,22	Skewness	-0,53
Range	4,00	Range	4,00	Range	4,00	Range	4,00	Range	4,00
Minimum	1,00	Minimum	1,00	Minimum	1,00	Minimum	1,00	Minimum	1,00
Maximum	5,00	Maximum	5,00	Maximum	5,00	Maximum	5,00	Maximum	5,00
Sum	547,00	Sum	663,00	Sum	619,00	Sum	660,00	Sum	723,00
Count	205,00	Count	205,00	Count	205,00	Count	205,00	Count	205,00

Fashion involvement. Question 17

111

	Product inv.	Purchase decision inv.	Purchase decision inv.	Social approval motives	Social approval motives	Sensory pleasure motives	Functional motives
Mean	2,90	3,82	2,71	3,04	2,73	3,07	4,22
Standard Err	0,09	0,07	0,08	0,08	0,07	0,09	0,07
Median	3,00	4,00	3,00	3,00	3,00	3,00	4,00
Mode	3,00	4,00	3,00	3,00	3,00	3,00	5,00
Standard Dev	1,23	1,07	1,12	1,21	1,06	1,23	0,94
Sample Vari	1,50	1,14	1,25	1,47	1,12	1,51	0,88
Kurtosis	-0,84	0,08	-0,72	-0,83	-0,55	-0,86	1,78
Skewness	0,08	-0,75	0,11	-0,01	0,14	-0,08	-1,33
Range	4,00	4,00	4,00	4,00	4,00	4,00	4,00
Minimum	1,00	1,00	1,00	1,00	1,00	1,00	1,00
Maximum	5,00	5,00	5,00	5,00	5,00	5,00	5,00
Sum	594,00	784,00	555,00	623,00	559,00	629,00	866,00
Count	205,00	205,00	205,00	205,00	205,00	205,00	205,00

Appendix 5. Test on statistically significant differences between "critics" and "joiners/spectators" behavioral groups

Group Statistics

	Technographics	N	Mean	Std. Deviation	Std. Error Mean
SocialMediaInvolvement	2 (Critics)	43	3,2765	,51684	,07882
	5 (Joiners/spectators)	42	3,2698	,48967	,07556
Motives Reviews	2	43	3,58	1,074	,164
	5	42	3,40	1,127	,174
Motives contests	2	43	3,88	1,051	,160
	5	42	3,57	1,192	,184
Motives community	2	43	2,77	,922	,141
	5	42	2,43	1,129	,174
Motives customer service	2	43	3,47	,984	,150
	5	42	2,95	1,268	,196
Motives submit ideas	2	43	2,88	,823	,125
	5	42	2,62	1,188	,183
Motives discounts	2	43	3,84	1,022	,156
	5	42	3,76	1,122	,173
Motives Excl info	2	43	3,42	1,096	,167
	5	42	3,29	1,088	,168
Motives learning	2	43	3,70	,887	,135
	5	42	3,71	,944	,146
Information on sales and discounts	2	43	7,72	2,004	,306
	5	42	7,43	2,520	,389
Experts ideas	2	43	6,65	2,080	,317
	5	42	6,31	2,682	,414
new products	2	43	7,12	2,038	,311

	5	42	6,81	2,422	,374
behind scenes	2	43	6,23	2,525	,385
	5	42	5,31	2,736	,422
Problems	2	43	6,67	2,368	,361
	5	42	5,98	2,627	,405

		Levene's Test for Equality of Variances		t-test for Equality of Means					95% Confidence Interval of the Difference	
		F	Sig.	T	df	Sig. (2-tailed)	Mean Differen ce	Std. Error Differen ce	Lower	Upp er
SocialMedial nvolvement	Equal variances assumed	,172	,680	,061	83	,952	,00664	,10925	-,21066	,223 95
	Equal variances not assumed			,061	82,92 5	,952	,00664	,10918	-,21052	,223 81
Motives Reviews	Equal variances assumed	,105	,747	,740	83	,462	,177	,239	-,298	,652
	Equal variances not assumed			,739	82,57 0	,462	,177	,239	-,299	,652
Motives contests	Equal variances assumed	,239	,626	1,282	83	,204	,312	,244	-,172	,797
	Equal variances not assumed			1,280	81,20 1	,204	,312	,244	-,173	,798
Motives community	Equal variances assumed	4,229	,043	1,517	83	,133	,339	,223	-,105	,783
	Equal variances not assumed			1,514	79,04 2	,134	,339	,224	-,107	,784
Motives customer service	Equal variances assumed	,468	,496	2,085	83	,040	,513	,246	,024	1,00 2
	Equal variances not assumed			2,079	77,32 6	,041	,513	,247	,022	1,00 4

Motives submit ideas	Equal variances assumed	10,218	,002	1,196	83	,235	,265	,221	-,175	,705
	Equal variances not assumed			1,191	72,790	,237	,265	,222	-,178	,707
Motives discounts	Equal variances assumed	,094	,760	,324	83	,747	,075	,233	-,387	,538
	Equal variances not assumed			,323	81,881	,747	,075	,233	-,388	,539
Motives Excl info	Equal variances assumed	,002	,969	,561	83	,576	,133	,237	-,338	,604
	Equal variances not assumed			,561	82,977	,576	,133	,237	-,338	,604
Motives learning	Equal variances assumed	,005	,944	-,084	83	,934	-,017	,199	-,412	,379
	Equal variances not assumed			-,084	82,390	,934	-,017	,199	-,412	,379
Information on sales and discounts	Equal variances assumed	2,548	,114	,593	83	,555	,292	,493	-,689	1,273
	Equal variances not assumed			,591	78,180	,556	,292	,495	-,692	1,277
Experts ideas	Equal variances assumed	5,457	,022	,657	83	,513	,342	,520	-,693	1,376
	Equal variances not assumed			,655	77,287	,514	,342	,521	-,697	1,380
new products	Equal variances assumed	2,049	,156	,632	83	,529	,307	,485	-,658	1,271
	Equal variances not assumed			,631	79,978	,530	,307	,486	-,660	1,274
behind scenes	Equal variances assumed	,793	,376	1,617	83	,110	,923	,571	-,212	2,058
	Equal variances not assumed			1,615	82,110	,110	,923	,571	-,214	2,060
Problems	Equal variances assumed	1,137	,289	1,288	83	,201	,698	,542	-,380	1,777
	Equal variances not assumed			1,286	81,676	,202	,698	,543	-,382	1,778

Appendix 6. Correlations between two dependent variables

Correlations

			SocialMediaInvolvement	FashionInvolvement
Spearman's rho	SocialMediaInvolvement	Correlation Coefficient	1,000	,255**
		Sig. (2-tailed)	.	,000
		N	205	205
	FashionInvolvement	Correlation Coefficient	,255**	1,000
		Sig. (2-tailed)	,000	.
		N	205	205

**. Correlation is significant at the 0.01 level (2-tailed).

Druck: KN Digital Printforce GmbH · Schockenriedstraße 37 · 70565 Stuttgart